Lifeline

BIOGRAPHIES

ADELE
Soul Music's Magical Voice

by Matt Doeden

Twenty-First Century Books · Minneapolis

Twenty-First Century Books
A division of Lerner Publishing Group, Inc.
241 First Avenue North
Minneapolis, MN 55401 U.S.A.

Website address: www.lernerbooks.com

Library of Congress Cataloging-in-Publication Data

Doeden, Matt.
    Adele : soul music's magical voice / by Matt Doeden.
        p.   cm. — (USA Today lifeline biographies)
    Includes bibliographical references and index.
    ISBN 978–1–4677–0808–1 (lib. bdg. : alk. paper)
    1. Adele, 1988– —Juvenile literature. 2. Singers—England—Biography—Juvenile literature. I. Title.
    ML3930.A165D64 2013
    782.42164092—dc23 [B]   2012027047

Manufactured in the United States of America
1 – CG – 12/31/12

USA TODAY A GANNETT COMPANY **Lifeline** BIOGRAPHIES

INTRODUCTION

Back on the red carpet: Adele arrives at the 2012 Grammy Awards in a sparkly black Giorgio Armani gown.

Triumphant Return

The Staples Center in Los Angeles, California, was packed on February 12, 2012, for the 54th Annual Grammy Awards. All of the music industry's biggest names were in attendance. Artists, producers, record executives, and the who's who of Hollywood were there to honor the best of pop music.

One name stood above all others: Adele Adkins—better known simply as Adele. Just three years before, few had even known her name. Since then, two smash albums had vaulted her to superstardom. Fans and fellow artists praised her for her powerful, soulful voice and intimate, lyrics.

Adele's talent wasn't the only reason all eyes were on her at the Grammys. Adele was returning to the world of music after having undergone surgery to remove a polyp (growth) from her vocal cords in 2011. As a result of the surgery, Adele had to cancel all her tour dates for the rest of the year. She couldn't talk for weeks. Many fans worried that she'd never get her singing voice back.

But Adele had worked hard. She rehabilitated her voice, just as an athlete rehabilitates an injured muscle or tendon. She was determined to come back, better than ever. And she knew exactly where she wanted to make her big return: the 2012 Grammys. The day had

IN F⊙CUS

The Grammys

Every year, the Grammy Awards program is one of the biggest celebrations of music in the United States. The National Academy of Recording Arts and Sciences of the United States awards the prestigious Grammy to recognize outstanding achievement in the music industry.

The Grammy Awards started in 1959. The awards are named for the gramophone, the forerunner to the phonograph (record player). Winners in each category receive a gold-plated trophy depicting a gramophone. The Grammys are awarded for a wide range of categories and musical styles. The biggest awards each year include Album of the Year, Record of the Year (for a single song), and Best New Artist.

come. Was she ready? Would her famous vocal power and control still be there?

Back Onstage

When Adele stepped onto the stage, she left no doubts about her recovery. She sang her smash hit "Rolling in the Deep," opening in an a cappella (vocals only) style. As the audience clapped along to the beat, she continued as her stripped-down background music kicked in. It was just Adele and the music, and she was in total control. The audience rose to their feet, roaring their approval as the music faded away. Adele stood at the center of the stage, soaking it up. It was the biggest ovation of the night.

And it only got better. Adele was nominated for six awards that night. Again and again and again—for all six nominations—presenters read out her name. *And the Grammy goes to . . . Adele.* Few music stars have enjoyed a night quite like that.

Handful: Adele poses with her six Grammy Awards in 2012.

Adele gracefully accepted the trophy for best pop solo performance for her song "Someone Like You." She was humble and gave credit to those who had brought her back. "Seeing as it's a vocal performance, I need to thank my doctors . . . who brought my voice back," she said. Her fans could breathe a sigh of relief. Adele *was* back.

Young Adele: Adele helps in the kitchen. Adele grew up in Tottenham, England.

Fascinated by Voices

■■■■

Adele Laurie Blue Adkins was born on May 5, 1988, in Tottenham, a neighborhood in London, England. Her mother, Penny, was only eighteen when Adele was born. Her father, Mark Evans, didn't stay with his young family for long. He left Penny when Adele was three years old. But Evans says he's at least partly responsible for shaping Adele's musical future. He remembers lying on the couch with his baby daughter, listening to music. Some of it was blues music. In fact, Evans says that his love of the blues inspired one of Adele's middle names.

Adele says that not having her dad around was never a big deal for her. "I don't feel like I'm missing anything," she said. "Some people make a big deal about coming from a single-parent family, but I know loads of people who grew up without having their dads around."

Adele also says that she never felt like an only child. Her mom came from a big family, so she always had aunts, uncles, and cousins around. "Mom's side is massive," she said. "All brilliant. Dominated by women and all really helping each other out, so even though she brought me up on her own, it was kind of a team effort."

Little Adele was fascinated by voices, including her own. She loved to sing, and she imitated her favorite artists. One of these was a British soul singer called Gabrielle, who had grown up near Adele's home. Penny, a big music fan herself, encouraged her daughter. She constantly played music in the house. She took Adele to her first concert at the age of three.

Soul singer: British star Gabrielle performs at the Royal Albert Hall in London, England, in 2008. She was one of young Adele's favorite artists.

British band: In 1991 Adele saw the Cure in concert. The group included members *(clockwise from bottom left)* guitarist Porl Thompson, drummer Boris William, bass player Simon Gallup, keyboardist Roger O'Donnel, and singer Robert Smith. The band had an influence on Adele's music.

They saw the Cure—a band that would remain a big influence on Adele. Penny also loved to have Adele sing for friends. She would dress her up, make a little stage, and let her sing away.

Tottenham Girl

As a child, Adele dreamed of being a fashion designer. Or a reporter. After her grandfather died of heart disease, she decided that she wanted to be a heart surgeon so she could help others like him. But music moved her and made her feel connected to people all over the world.

"When I was a girl, I loved love songs," she later remembered. "I always loved the ones about horrible relationships. One that you could really relate to and made you cry."

Adele grew up in Tottenham. It had once been a bustling blue-collar, working-class neighborhood. By the time Adele was a child, it was a poverty-stricken area. But it also offered a great deal of diversity. Adele was one of the only white children in her class at school. She credits her black friends with helping her learn to love soul music—a style with roots in communities of African descent.

Adele and her mother left Tottenham when she was nine. They moved to Brighton in southern England. Two years later, they settled in the Brixton district of London. But Adele always considered herself a Tottenham girl.

Childhood neighborhood: Adele grew up in this home in Tottenham, London.

New neighborhood: At one point, after moving out of Tottenham, Adele lived with her mom, Penny, in an apartment in this building in London.

Evolving Tastes

Adele listened to all sorts of music. She loved the Spice Girls, Lauryn Hill, and just about anything that was popular during the late 1990s and early 2000s. But her tastes began to change when she was a teenager. One day in a record store, she wandered into the jazz section. The store was featuring a sale on greatest hits CDs from legendary jazz singers Ella Fitzgerald and Etta James. Adele bought both. Later, when she popped them into her CD player, she was mesmerized. It was unlike anything she'd ever heard.

"When I heard the [Etta James] song 'Fool That I Am,' everything changed for me," she later said.

Jazz offered Adele something other styles didn't. Ella's and Etta's sound was smooth, laid back, and easy to listen to. The songs had a depth, both musically and lyrically, that was missing in a lot of pop music of the time. With Ella and Etta, there was often just a singer, a piano, and a story. Adele was hooked. She knew that music was what she wanted to do with her life.

IN F◉CUS

Jazz

Jazz is a major influence on Adele's style. Jazz is a music style that grew out of blues in the early 1900s. At first, jazz was mainly dance music, popular mostly in African American communities. But later, it became known best for its free-flowing, improvisational (unplanned) style and gained a more widespread, diverse audience. Jazz musicians famously play off one another, straying from set melodies, returning, then straying again. Much of jazz is instrumental. Vocalists such as Ella Fitzgerald, Billie Holiday, and Nat King Cole have made their mark on the genre.

Musical Influence: Ella Fitzgerald

Ella Fitzgerald—known as the Queen of Jazz and the First Lady of Song—was born on April 25, 1917, in Newport News, Virginia. Her mother died when she was a teenager, and Ella's stepfather was abusive. So she left home. She ended up working as a lookout at a bordello (house of prostitution), keeping an eye out for police. She was eventually arrested and sent to the Colored Orphan Asylum in the Bronx, New York. She was later moved to a reformatory from which she escaped, living on the streets.

Fitzgerald had one big thing going for her—her voice. She was blessed with a range and control that most professional singers only dream of. She entered an amateur night contest at the famous Apollo Theater in Harlem, an African American neighborhood in New York. She won. Bandleader Chick Webb was impressed by her voice. He invited her to record with him, and her career was off and running.

Fitzgerald would remain a major figure in the jazz music scene for the next six decades. Her hits include "A-Tisket, A-Tasket," "Love for Sale," and "Mack the Knife." She suffered from diabetes late in life and lost her sight and both legs. Fitzgerald died in 1996. She left a lasting legacy and continues to inspire countless new music stars—including Adele.

Queen of Jazz: Ella Fitzgerald (*left*) collaborated with some of the greatest popular musicians of the 1900s, including trumpeter Louis Armstrong, guitarist Joe Pass, and bandleaders Count Basie and Duke Ellington.

IN FOCUS

Musical Influence: Etta James

From the moment Adele first heard Etta James's warm, passionate voice, she was captivated. Adele said that James was the first singer who ever made her stop what she was doing and sit down. She just had to listen without distractions.

James, born in Los Angeles, California, in 1938, rose to fame in the early 1960s. She sang in a wide range of styles and is best known for her interpretation of the blues and R & B. Some music experts credit her with bridging R & B and rock. Her recordings of the songs "At Last" and "I'd Rather Go Blind" have become classics, covered time and again by a wide variety of musicians.

James struggled with success, however. She became addicted to the drug heroin and turned to petty crime to support her habit. The destructive influence of the addiction took a toll on her music career. James eventually went to a rehab center and got clean. She made a comeback in the 1990s, performing with her sons, Donto and Sametto. She died of cancer in 2012.

James was inducted into the Rock and Roll Hall of Fame in 1993. In 2008 *Rolling Stone* magazine ranked her 22nd on its list of the Top 100 Singers of All Time.

A warm voice: Etta James records a song at Fame Studios in Alabama in 1967. James is known for bridging R & B and rock.

January 23, 2012

Etta James: 10 Songs That Defined Her Career and Sound

<u>From the Pages of</u>
<u>USA TODAY</u>

The career of Etta James, who died Friday at age 73, spanned six decades, during which she put her fiery stamp on a broad range of R & B, blues and jazz songs.
USA TODAY's *Steve Jones recommends a small sampling from her extensive catalog:*

"The Wallflower (Dance with Me Henry)." James' career started in 1955 with this rocking answer to Hank Ballard's "Work with Me Annie." The tune, which James recorded with the trio The Peaches, went to No. 1 on both the R&B and pop charts.

"At Last." This romantic ballad with its gorgeous strings became her signature song (Beyoncé sang it at President Obama's [2008] Inaugural Ball) and it was a No. 2 R & B hit in 1961. It had been a top 10 pop hit for Glenn Miller in 1942.

"All I Could Do Was Cry." A regretful James watches as her former lover walks down the aisle with another woman. James slowly wells with emotion on this 1960 track, which was a No. 2 R & B hit.

"Tell Mama." This horn-fueled 1967 burner promises "to make everything all right" for a man who has been kicked to the curb by his previous lover. It was James' last top 10 hit, and it had the potent lost-love classic "I'd Rather Go Blind" on the B-side.

"All the Way Down." This funky, horn-kissed 1973 song about the allure of the streets was a change of pace for James and reflected the social themes that were influential at that time.

"Feel Like Breakin' Up Somebody's Home." Etta's in a salty mood with a lover who has another on this Albert King cover from 1990's *Seven Year Itch.*

"This Bitter Earth." *Blue Gardenia*, her acclaimed album of jazz standards with pianist Cedar Walton, included this 1960 song made famous by Dinah Washington.

"Cigarettes and Coffee." James released her final album, *The Dreamer*, in November and included this simmering rendition of an Otis Redding cover.

"Love's Been Rough on Me." The poignant, reflective title track from her 1997 album of the same name brims with emotion.

"Somebody to Love." A sassy James gets to rocking on this Delbert McClinton-written jam from 2003's *Let's Roll.*

—Steve Jones

High school: Adele went to the BRIT School, which focuses on performing arts, especially music. The school is one of the few performing arts institutions in Britain that is free to attend.

The BRIT School

Adele had an idea about her life's dream. But she didn't feel empowered to make it happen. She lacked confidence in herself and often didn't even feel as if a singing career was possible. She felt trapped in schools where nobody encouraged her. So when she was fourteen, she applied to the London School for Performing Arts & Technology (better known as the BRIT School, or just the BRIT). This public school focuses on the performing arts, most notably music. When Adele applied, only about one applicant in three actually was accepted to the school. Adele made the cut.

The change in atmosphere was dramatic. Adele no longer felt stifled and held back. She was finally in a school where she felt encouraged and where she was surrounded by students with similar ambitions. She got to focus on music and technology almost all day. "I could just listen to music every day for four years," she said. "I felt . . . alive. They taught us to be open-minded and we were really encouraged to write our own music. . . . I took it very seriously."

At first, she wasn't planning to pursue a career as a singer. Instead, she hoped to make it in some other aspect of the music business—perhaps in recording or producing music. Adele studied many of the technical aspects of the industry. She learned to do sound checks for instruments, amplifiers, and microphones. She studied the ins and outs of recording a demo (self-recorded song made to be sent to record companies). Yet she still had self-doubts.

"I always knew I would be involved in music," she later said of her life's goals at the time. "But I thought I would be a receptionist or work in a shop and then, on my days off, I would go and play a little acoustic [music without electronic instruments] show for my family and friends. I didn't even bother to really seriously dream about being a singer. Everyone I knew had dreams and none of theirs had come true. So why...would mine?"

Adele was popular during her years at the BRIT School. Her classmates remembered her as fun and outgoing. Pop star Jessie J was at the school at the same time as Adele.

Classmate: Adele attended the BRIT School with stars such as Jessie J, seen here performing in London in 2012.

The BRIT School

The London School for Performing Arts & Technology—better known as the BRIT School—is a high school in London. It is devoted to preparing students for futures in the arts, especially in the recording arts. The school was founded in 1991 and is partially supported by private business donations. A large part of the school's funding comes from the earnings of the BRIT Awards, one of the biggest music award shows in Britain.

The idea for the BRIT School came out of the 1980 film *Fame*. London-based educator and entrepreneur Mark Featherstone-Witty imagined a real-world school like the one in the movie. In such a school, students could prepare for music careers. He approached Richard Branson, owner of Virgin Records, with the idea. Branson agreed to sponsor the project, as did the British Phonographic Industry (BPI). Early in the school's history, critics argued that it had produced few music successes. That changed in the 2000s. Amy Winehouse, Katy B, Leona Lewis, Imogen Heap, and Adele are just a few of the school's famous success stories. Their achievements have helped increase interest in the school, which announced plans to expand in 2012.

BRIT stars: Leona Lewis performs at the Royal Albert Hall in London in 2012. Leona attended the BRIT School, as did singers such as Amy Winehouse and Adele.

"We used to jam at lunch time and someone would play guitar and we both would just sing," Jessie remembered. "At school, she was kind of loud and everyone knew her and she was the girl everyone loved and up for a laugh and you could hear her laugh from a mile down the corridor."

Adele also made an impact on the school's administrators. Liz Penney, the school's director, remembered Adele as a student. "Sometimes she worked really hard and sometimes she didn't work quite so hard," Penney said. "She was quite chatty, but she always made me laugh. From the time she came here—when some of the other students weren't so into songwriting—she was [a songwriter] from the moment she arrived."

Some of Adele's friends encouraged her to pursue a singing career. But Adele was still filled with self-doubt. "I never thought my being a professional singer was going to happen," she said. "So I sometimes thought [trying to become a singer] was a waste of time."

The start: Adele performs on stage in 2007. Adele wouldn't have gotten to the stage without the help of a friend who posted her songs on MySpace in 2006.

Chasing the Dream

By her final year at the BRIT School, Adele was no longer seeking a behind-the-scenes career. She was convinced that she had what it took to become a vocalist. Part of her inspiration had come from the recording artist Pink. She had seen Pink perform and was impressed. "I had never heard, being in the room, someone sing like that live," she later said. "I remember sort of feeling like I was in a wind tunnel, her voice just hitting me. It was incredible."

Adele's ambition was growing. But she was still in high school and didn't really know how to make her dream come true. So she continued her studies at the BRIT School, focusing on her classes.

In one class, students had to record demos. For this project, Adele recorded several songs she wrote herself. When the class was done, she didn't know what to do with the songs. She gave them to her friends to listen to. They were impressed. And they had an idea about how to get Adele's name—and her music—out to the public.

Going Online

For years the music industry had been struggling with how the Internet could be used to rapidly share music with listeners. Many music executives knew that the Internet was a vehicle for music to be pirated—illegally copied and distributed. Large record labels pushed back with lawsuits. Yet at the same time, some indie artists (artists not attached to a record label) and small record labels embraced

Influence: Pink performs at the Grammy Awards in 2010. Adele saw her perform in concert and knew she, too, had to be a vocalist.

the Internet. They saw its possibilities and recognized the Internet as a place where unknown recording artists could be heard. Artists would no longer have to rely on record labels to decide who should and could be popular. These artists could publish and distribute their own music and let music fans decide.

One of Adele's friends was handy with computers. In 2006 he posted three of her songs on MySpace, a social networking site. In addition, an online music publication included two of Adele's songs—"Daydreamer" and "My Same"—on its site.

Adele didn't really expect anything to come of this online exposure.

IN F●CUS

Musical Influence: Pink

As a teenager, Adele had seen pop-R & B artist Pink perform in concert. Adele said the experience changed her and inspired her to follow her dream of becoming a singer.

Alecia Beth Moore, who goes by the stage name Pink, was born on September 8, 1979, in Doylestown, Pennsylvania. She always wanted to be a singer. She was writing her own songs by the age of fourteen. At the age of sixteen, she formed the R & B band Choice with two friends. The band gained the attention of record producer Antonio "L.A." Reid. He encouraged Pink to pursue a solo career. She followed his advice. Her debut album, *Can't Take Me Home*, was released in 2000.

Pink felt that the sound of her first album was too mainstream and too geared to pop. She wanted to be a singer-songwriter, not just a pop star. She achieved that feel with her second album, *Missundaztood* (2001). Adele lists this album as one of her favorites. It featured several hit singles, most notably "Get the Party Started." The song helped make Pink an international star and a major force in pop and R & B. Over the next ten years, she released one hit album after another. In 2009 *Billboard* ranked her the top pop artist of the decade.

September 6, 2006

MySpace Butts into iTunes' Turf

From the Pages of
USA TODAY

Apple rules digital music, but will it be able to fight off an assault from the hot social network MySpace?

Tech analysts and Apple enthusiast websites expect Apple, which has a 70% share of digital music sales, to unveil a new iPod player next week that can sync with movies at its iTunes online store.

On Tuesday, meanwhile, MySpace began offering unsigned bands a way to sell their music directly to fans online. The songs are being sold in unprotected MP3 format, a bonus for consumers who have been frustrated with purchasing copy-protected songs that wouldn't play on some devices.

"MySpace isn't a threat to iTunes now, but over time, it could become one," says Phil Leigh, an analyst with Inside Digital Media. "Their audience is so huge, and growing. I can see the major labels signing on to do this eventually." MySpace has nearly 50 million monthly visitors in the USA, according to measurement firm Nielsen/NetRatings.

MySpace CEO Chris DeWolfe says his goal is to have the largest online music store. "We're the biggest music site now," he says. "Converting to the biggest music store would be a natural progression."

MySpace is working with tech firm Snocap, which is providing the tools to sell the songs online. The tools work not just with MySpace, but also any website, blog or even an e-mail.

Unsigned artists go through many hoops to have their music sold at iTunes or Amazon. For this, they simply register at snocap.com, and upload their songs. Then they are given the tools to cut and paste the computer code for selling their music onto a website or blog. By the end of the year, MySpace plans to make it even easier: Click a button or two at MySpace, and an instant online store can be generated directly there.

Snocap and MySpace take a cut of 45 cents per song, and leave the pricing decisions to the artist.

Meanwhile, all eyes are on Apple's announcement Tuesday about its new products. Gene Munster, an analyst at Piper Jaffray, expects it to confirm a long-awaited addition to iTunes: movie downloads. "For the consumer, this will be as big of a deal as the opening of the iTunes store," he says. "People have been asking for movie downloads for years."

—Jefferson Graham

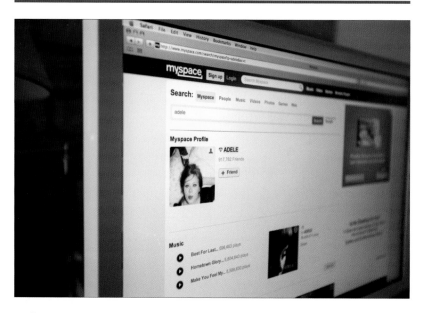

Online: Adele's MySpace page *(above)* is a frequently visited site. Adele gained fans because of her MySpace page, which also led to her first recording contract.

But it was fun to see her music online, and it was easy to do. So she figured it was worth a shot.

In May 2006, Adele graduated from the BRIT School and began to prepare to go to college. It was a difficult decision to make. Adele's mother wanted her daughter to attend the University of Liverpool. Penny reasoned that going to Liverpool (about 200 miles, or 322 kilometers, from London) would help Adele learn to be on her own. But Adele didn't want to leave London. She wanted to study at the University of London. The disagreement between mother and daughter inspired Adele to write the song "Hometown Glory." "It was just four chords on the guitar and pressing one string," Adele said of the song. "I played it as a protest song to my mother. It basically said, 'This is why I'm staying [in London].'"

In the meantime, Adele had been wrong to assume that nothing would come of putting her songs on MySpace. People *were* listening. The word spread quickly. She was getting messages from people who loved her songs. And then she got an e-mail from someone claiming to represent a record label. At first, she didn't even believe that the message was genuine. "I thought, 'Yeah, whatever.' I didn't believe you could get signed [to a record label contract] through MySpace."

Once again, Adele was wrong.

Signing with XL

XL Recordings, based out of London, is known as a record label that takes chances. An executive with the label heard "Hometown Glory" on MySpace. He loved the sound and the song's political message (uniting against government control). The song fit perfectly with the kind of music that XL produced. The label sent the e-mail to Adele, inviting her to its studios for a meeting. At first, Adele ignored the message. She hadn't heard of XL and didn't know whether the invitation was for real. When she finally did respond in the spring of 2006, she expected that she would be offered an internship (entry-level position with little or no pay). She took a friend with her to the meeting, because she wasn't sure whether she should even trust that the invitation had come from an actual record label.

The label: XL Recordings represents popular artists such as Adele, The xx, and Jack White.

XL Recordings

XL Recordings is a small, independent record label based out of London. Richard Russell, Tim Palmer, and Nick Halkes founded the company in 1989 as a label for dance music. Palmer and Halkes left the label during the 1990s, leaving Russell to give it direction. Russell expanded the label and began releasing more rock and pop. He encouraged music with a political message.

One of XL's earliest successes was the electronic dance band the Prodigy. The band's 1994 album *Music for the Jilted Generation* with the XL label went to the top spot on British charts. Other major artists to work with XL have included the White Stripes, Radiohead, and Thom Yorke (Radiohead's lead singer, who released his debut solo album through XL in 2006).

Then came Adele. Her sudden stardom vaulted XL to a new level of success. Her first two albums were among the best-selling in British history. XL was no longer just a small record label. In 2012, at the Music Week Awards in London, XL was honored as Label of the Year.

XL artists: Even though XL is a small record label, it has had many success stories. Some of those are Keith Flint of the Prodigy (*left*) and Thom Yorke of Radiohead (*right*).

XL was the real deal. It wasn't the biggest label in the business, but it had enjoyed a fair share of success. And the representative with whom Adele met shocked her with a surprise offer. They didn't suggest she take an internship with the label. Instead, they wanted to sign her to a recording contract!

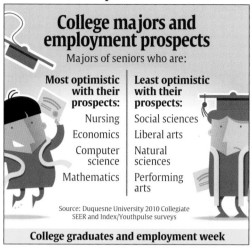

USA TODAY Snapshots®

College majors and employment prospects

Majors of seniors who are:

Most optimistic with their prospects:	Least optimistic with their prospects:
Nursing	Social sciences
Economics	Liberal arts
Computer science	Natural sciences
Mathematics	Performing arts

Source: Duquesne University 2010 Collegiate SEER and Index/Youthpulse surveys

College graduates and employment week

By Jae Yang and Paul Trap, USA TODAY, 2010

Of course, the label wanted to make sure Adele was really the one who had sung the demos. So XL arranged a small concert for her soon after the meeting. Adele took the stage and left no doubts. It was her voice. XL founder Richard Russell knew he had discovered something special. "She had an extremely strong idea of what she wanted to do," he said. "I don't think you get that [vision] from the BRIT School. You get that when you have great instincts. . . . There's something about her voice. It connects to you very directly. Her subject matter—being hurt—she talks about it in a way that's so easy to relate to. It's very honest."

Adele and XL agreed to a recording contract in September 2006. Adele was just eighteen years old.

Overcoming Doubt

The amount of money Adele would earn through her contract with XL wasn't huge. The terms of the contract were modest. XL wasn't ready to instantly promote Adele as the next great star of the music world. She would need to prove herself first. The first step would be to write enough songs for an album. And the label didn't exactly see eye-to-eye with Adele on what the direction of that album should be.

Adele later explained the differences in vision. "When XL signed me, I think they thought I was going to be an acoustic artist," she said. "At the time, I had no choice but to be an acoustic artist because I didn't have the money to have a band. I really wanted to be a pop star. I think they thought I was going to be more low-key than I would become."

None of that really mattered until Adele actually had material to record. The writing process didn't start out well. So far, Adele had written only three songs that were fit for an album. She was overwhelmed by the idea of writing an entire album's worth of music—roughly ten to fifteen songs. As weeks and months passed, she still hadn't been able to write anything new. Her confidence was lower than ever. The feelings of self-doubt that she had so successfully overcome at the BRIT School were coming back.

The small screen: Adele performs on the British late-night music television show *Later...with Jools Holland* in 2007.

Adele needed a shot of confidence. It came in June 2007. She was invited to appear on the British late-night television show *Later...with Jools Holland.* Hosted by musician Jools Holland, the show is all about music. It covers a wide range of genres, from pop to soul to jazz. It features a mix of famous artists and unknowns—and that was where Adele fit in. One of the show's producers had heard and liked one of Adele's demos. The show invited her to perform even though she had not released an album yet.

It was an exciting invitation for Adele. She and her mother had been fans of the show and had watched it together many times. It was a big deal. The other singers who would join her on that episode were Iceland's Björk and former Beatle Paul McCartney. Adele would get to sit beside and meet the two famous artists. She said she couldn't stop crying afterward.

On the show, Adele was nervous, and it showed during her per-formance. But even with her nervousness, her talent came through. Reporters reviewed her performance favorably. And more than half a million television viewers had seen her sing on the show. It was by far the most exposure she had ever had. And it was just what she needed to get past the writer's block that was holding her back.

Gaining popularity: Adele poses for a photo shoot in 2008, the same year she released her first album, *19*.

A Taste of Fame

After appearing on *Later...with Jools Holland*, Adele was back on track. She was writing songs again. In the style that would make her famous, she tapped into her life story for inspiration. Her lyrics were honest and heartfelt. Many of her songs described pain, hurt, and anger from failed relationships. They were exactly the kinds of songs that she had been drawn to in her younger years. She could only hope that her stories would touch listeners in the same way.

"Hometown Glory"

Adele recorded most of her debut album in the summer of 2007. Her label, Pacemaker (part of XL Recordings), planned for the album to be released in 2008. In the meantime, Adele's name was still fresh in fans' minds from her big TV appearance. XL didn't want to wait half a year to capitalize on that name recognition. This meant that the label needed to give fans something from Adele much sooner. So in October 2007, Pacemaker issued a vinyl-only release of "Hometown Glory." The B side (song on the opposite side of the record) was a cover of Etta James's "Fool That I Am." It was a song that had been important to Adele in her early teens. Releasing this song was a way for her to honor James's `influence on her music.

"It was a song that just changed everything for me," Adele explained. "It inspired me to want to write my own songs, to be honest and to try to touch people. Basically, I think it's a beautiful song. I love singing it. . . . And so I thought it would be nice for my fans if I included it on this single."

Nobody at XL had really expected much out of the "Hometown Glory" record. But the song took off. Radio stations across the United Kingdom picked it up before it was even formally released.

Record release: XL Recordings released the song "Hometown Glory" on vinyl in 2007 to keep Adele's name in people's minds. The record was rereleased later and can be purchased in MP3 format.

IN F✚CUS

Musical Influence: The Spice Girls

As a teenager, Adele was devoted to the British girl band the Spice Girls, which formed in 1994. Each member took on a personality and a name to match. Adele's favorite Spice Girl was Geri Halliwell—better known as Ginger Spice. Other members included Victoria Adams (Posh Spice), Melanie Brown (Scary Spice), Emma Bunton (Baby Spice), and Melanie Chisholm (Sporty Spice).

The Spice Girls were all about image. Some music critics argue that their marketing was more important than their talent. But that mattered little to their hoards of young fans—including Adele. The Spice Girls represented "girl power."

They weren't ashamed to use their good looks to advance their careers. They embraced their roles as sex symbols. They used that image to sell millions of albums and to earn lots of money.

Spice Girls' hits include 1996's "Wannabe" and "2 Become 1" and 1998's "Spice Up Your Life." The group declined in popularity after Halliwell left the band in 1998. Almost ten years later, in 2007, the group reunited. Tickets for the reunion tour sold out in thirty-eight seconds! Although the group's members have moved on to other pursuits, the Spice Girls remain one of the best-known pop bands of their era.

Girl power: The British girl group the Spice Girls sing during a reunion performance in 2007. Adele was a big fan of the group when she was a teen.

Britain's Radio 1 and Radio 2 stations both included it in their regular rotation of songs.

Although the song was popular on the radio, fans didn't have much opportunity to buy it in stores. XL had released it on a very limited basis, which meant it was hard to find. And since the charts rank songs based largely on sales, "Hometown Glory" had no chance to make it onto the charts. (Adele and XL would later give the song a broad release. It did go on to make the charts—boosted in part by being used on TV shows including *Skins*, *One Tree Hill*, and *Grey's Anatomy*.)

Great Expectations

Adele had begun to create quite a buzz in the music industry—all without releasing a single album. A British Broadcasting Company (BBC) survey of music critics revealed her as the artist expected to break out in 2008. And near the end of 2007, the BRIT Awards made a huge announcement. Adele would be chosen as the recipient of the BRIT's first Critic's Choice award in 2008. The award honors the artist most

Big announcement: British actor and DJ Reggie Yates *(right)* interviews Adele at the BRIT Awards nomination event in 2007. Adele went on to win the Critic's Choice award.

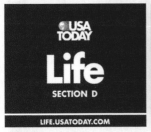

Digital album sales soar, but the CD isn't going away yet

From the Pages of
USA TODAY

Are digital album sales finally taking off? Just one week after Eminem's *Recovery* became the first album to sell 1 million digital copies, Adele's *21* has surpassed the milestone and is now the biggest-selling digital album in history.

Digital sales of *21* exceed 1.017 million (out of 2.6 million total), compared with *Recovery*'s 1.005 million (out of 3.9 million).

Overall, almost one-third (32%) of the 155.5 million albums sold in the first half of 2011 were digital, according to a midyear report released last week by Nielsen SoundScan. That's up 19% from the same period in 2010, when 27% of 153.9 million album sales were digital.

Adele is helping fuel the rapid growth in digital album sales overall, but "she's not just a digital phenomenon," says Keith Caulfield, *Billboard*'s associate director of charts/retail. "She appeals to older consumers, who will still buy full albums, and to younger people who may just buy a single track."

She also has sold more than 4 million copies of hit single "Rolling in the Deep," but "she connects with people in a way where they feel she is a 'full-package artist' and you want to hear everything she sings."

likely to break out in any given year. With this award, Adele felt the pressure of high expectations. That was a lot to live up to. Adele herself wasn't even sure what to expect from her debut album.

"I had no specific plans for my album," she said. "For me the album was just about making a record of songs to get a boy [former boyfriend] off my chest and include all the different kinds of music that

Caulfield says at least two more albums, Lady Gaga's *The Fame* (976,000) and Mumford & Sons' *Sigh No More* (890,000), probably will join the 1 million digital sales club by the year's end.

These days, music buyers have ever-increasing options for accessing music, including phones, computers and other electronic devices, as well as cloud and streaming services. Caulfield says the technology is moving at a faster pace than it did in the past, when the move from cassettes to CDs took more than a decade.

"If you ask anyone under the age of 20 how many CDs they have, they might look at you with a blank stare," he says. "This is completely normal and expected. Every day brings a new service or wrinkle to how people get their entertainment or music."

Physical CDs still make up two-thirds of all sales, so it's unlikely they'll disappear anytime soon. But Paul Resnikoff, publisher of Los Angeles-based *Digital Music News*, says he expects digital album sales to increase for the next three years before flattening out. He says CD sales will continue to decline as consumers get more comfortable with downloading and CDs get increasingly harder to find in stores.

"The reality is that digital formats have shown growth because they started from zero, but they haven't come close to replacing the physical totals of 10 years ago," Resnikoff says. "The problem hasn't been one of appetite. There is more access now than there has ever been in the history of music, but there hasn't been an ability to price that music.

"You can sit in front of YouTube for 12 hours a day and not pay a dime."

—Steve Jones

I love. So [on the album] there's pop; there's a bit of electro; there's jazz; there's folk; and of course there's soul. . . . It was simply that I got into a relationship that went very sour. . . . Apart from 'Hometown Glory,' 'Daydreamer,' and 'My Same,'—which were all written earlier, when I was between 16 and 18—the whole album is all about one boy."

Chasing a Hit

With the buzz surrounding Adele, Pacemaker released another Adele single, "Chasing Pavements," on December 7, 2007. It was the song that introduced Adele to the largest number of music fans yet. As with most of the tracks on the soon-to-be-released album, "Chasing Pavements" was about a relationship gone bad. Adele explained the unique song title. She'd written the song after getting into an argument with a boyfriend at a nightclub. She left the club upset and found herself running down the streets.

"There was no one chasing me, and I wasn't chasing anyone," she said. "I was just running away. I remember saying to myself, 'What you're chasing is empty pavement.'"

Music critics loved the song. Adele was getting more and more coverage in British music publications. Magazines were seeking interviews, music critics were predicting great things out of the soon-to-be-released album, and fans were wondering just who this young new voice in soul was. Adele was concerned with all the media buzz. It was coming before her first album had even been released. Adele wasn't as interested in what critics had to say as she was in what the fans would think. "I feel like I'm being shoved down everyone's throat," she told an interviewer. "My worst fear is my music won't connect with the public. Earlier this morning, because 'Chasing Pavements' went up for download [on iTunes] last night, just being adventurous I scrolled down to the last 30 of the top 100 on iTunes to see if it was there. And it wasn't there. It was No. 12! And that was only 9 o'clock!"

As her success on iTunes showed, Adele had no need to fear the reception from the public. "Chasing Pavements" was an instant hit. So was the music video, which featured the aftermath of a car crash in a London park. Fans loved Adele's unique voice and the vivid emotion that came through in her lyrics. So did fellow artists. R & B superstar Kanye West posted a link to the video on his blog, declaring it "dope." Thanks to plenty of word of mouth, "Chasing Pavements" enjoyed a long stay in the United Kingdom's top 40, peaking at number 2. Fans

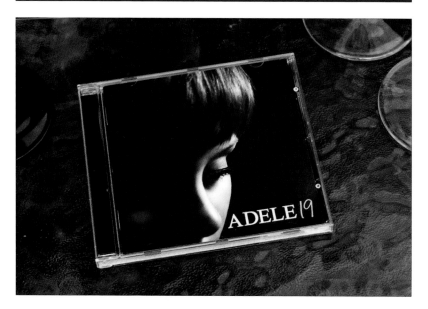

Debut: Adele's album *19* was released in January 2008. The name of the album refers to Adele's age at the time she recorded the songs.

begged for more, and they were about to get it.

19

Adele's debut album was finally released on January 28, 2008. It was titled *19*, the age at which Adele had recorded it. It included the three songs Adele had first put on MySpace, along with eight she'd written in 2007—at the age of nineteen. It also included a cover of the Bob Dylan song "Make You Feel My Love."

Fans were ready and eager to buy the new album. It debuted at number 1 on the UK charts. That was an amazing accomplishment for a debut album.

The critical reception to the album was overwhelmingly positive. A handful of critics gave Adele negative reviews. One reviewer described the music as emotionally vapid (empty), while another claimed, "There's precious little on the album that prevents it from collapsing under the weight of its own expectation. . . . For all the hype, Adele is not ready to produce an album of sufficient depth to match her voice."

But the good reviews outweighed the bad. Chris Long's review of *19* for the BBC website said, "Pitching up somewhere between blues, folk and jazz, she's included something for everyone without ever pandering to a particular trend. Her melodies exude [give off] warmth, her singing is occasionally stunning...."

Many reviewers compared Adele to singer Amy Winehouse. Their similar lyrical, jazzy approach to music and the fact that both had attended the BRIT School made the comparisons inevitable. But in the end, Adele really didn't sound much like Winehouse. Adele's sound was unique, and that's what made the album so appealing to fans.

BRIT singer: Some people compared Adele to performer Amy Winehouse *(above).* Both of them attended the BRIT School. Winehouse died in 2011.

USA TODAY Snapshots®

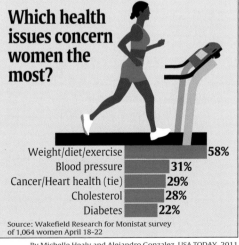

Which health issues concern women the most?

Weight/diet/exercise	58%
Blood pressure	31%
Cancer/Heart health (tie)	29%
Cholesterol	28%
Diabetes	22%

Source: Wakefield Research for Monistat survey of 1,064 women April 18–22

By Michelle Healy and Alejandro Gonzalez, USA TODAY, 2011

IN F⊕CUS

Image Isn't Everything

When Adele first hit the charts, her appearance was one of the first things people noticed about her. In modern pop music, looks are often as important as voice. Many fans expect female pop stars to look like models. But Adele didn't fit that mold. She had a more generous figure—not fat, but not thin either. Adele is pretty, though she does not have the looks of a supermodel.

Her appearance drew a range of responses. Some music fans and critics made fun of her weight and her casual style of dress. Others applauded her for looking like and being a real woman. They felt she represented a lot of real-world girls and women who needed to see role models who looked more like they did.

Adele lost weight after she came onto the music scene. But she says that was more for her health than because she wanted to change her image. She says that she isn't obsessed with appearance. "Being told how to look is about being a product, and I don't want to be a product," she explained. "I'd say my look is shabby-chic. I just wear big jumpers [blouses] over tight jeans and carry a huge bag and that's it. I don't want people to notice how I look. . . . I want people to just listen to me."

Just Adele: Adele has faced criticism for her casual style. She doesn't have supermodel looks, and in the early days of her career, she dressed in baggy yet comfortable clothes for her performances.

Dealing with Fame

Adele attended the 2008 BRIT Awards in London just a couple of weeks after *19* was released. She was there to accept her Critic's Choice award. It was both exciting and stressful for her. She was suddenly surrounded by the biggest names in the UK music business. Stars such as Paul McCartney, Leona Lewis, Rihanna, and the Arctic Monkeys were in attendance. Adele was being honored as a major talent, even though her debut album had been for sale in stores for only two weeks.

If all of that wasn't enough, British pop star Will Young—an artist whom Adele had adored as a girl—was on hand to introduce her. "This is a new BRIT award," Young told the audience. "It's given to an act that our most eminent [respected] critics believe will break through in 2008. This year's winner has already proven the critics right, because her debut album *19* went straight to number 1 in the album charts. It looks like it will stay at the top of the charts for a good long time."

Adele kept her acceptance speech short. She offered a few thank-yous and joked that she thought speeches were boring.

Inside, Adele was conflicted. She knew the award was a big honor and a huge boost to her young career. But she also felt strange about accepting it. Most

All smiles: Adele accepts the Critic's Choice award in February 2008.

artists got BRIT awards for being great. She'd gotten hers because people thought she *could* be great. She worried that people might think she didn't deserve it.

Adele felt trapped in some ways. She sometimes felt as if she'd been named a star without having really earned it. She worried that her fellow artists wouldn't respect her for that, and she wasn't sure how to deal with it. Learning how to deal with fame, especially at a young age, is extremely difficult. Only twenty years old, Adele would have to learn how to deal with the loss of privacy that comes with fans wanting autographs, photographers wanting photos, and the media scrutinizing her every move. The music industry is littered with artists who have achieved sudden fame at a young age and then burned out. Adele didn't want that. She hoped to be around for a long time. And yet, even though her album sales were soaring and her songs were everywhere, the pressures of fame made this a depressing time for Adele. She later admitted that she had had thoughts of suicide. A talk with a friend helped her realize that all the attention was a blessing. She just had to learn to adjust to her new way of life.

The Big Apple: Adele performs at an Apple Store in New York City in 2008. Adele said she was scared about coming to the United States to perform, because she wasn't sure whether U.S. fans would embrace her music.

Coming to America

In April 2008, Adele launched her first tour—An Evening with Adele—in the United Kingdom. She played shows in England, Wales, and Scotland to favorable reviews. She sang mostly songs from 19. She also mixed in a few covers, including "Fool That I Am," Sam Cooke's "That's It, I Quit, I'm Movin' On," and "Many Shades of Black" by the band the Raconteurs. And of course, she finished off every show with the song most fans wanted to hear—"Chasing Pavements." After eleven shows in the United Kingdom, it was time to take her show to the United States.

For a pop singer, no market is bigger and more important than the United States. British rock artists—from the Beatles and the Rolling Stones in the 1960s to twenty-first-century acts such as Coldplay and Muse—have enjoyed huge success in the United States. Adele was very popular in Britain by 2008. But that wasn't a guarantee that she would be a hit across the Atlantic Ocean. In fact, many British acts—both fan favorites and critical darlings—have flamed out in their attempts to bring their music to the United States. A sound that is popular in Britain doesn't always work with U.S. listeners.

Adele knew that success was no sure thing. "I was quite scared about heading over to America," she said. "I'm really British and I didn't really know if the music would work."

Adele did have one thing going for her. By 2008 music fans in the United States were on something of a British soul kick. British soul singers such as Amy Winehouse, Duffy, Joss Stone, and Corrine Bailey

Other Brits: British singer-songwriter Joss Stone performs at the Grammy Awards in 2005. Joss Stone, like Adele, is a British singer who is also popular in the United States.

Rae had all made an impact in the United States. Adele hoped to be next in line.

Across the Pond

Touring in the United States to promote her album *19*—which hadn't yet been released there—was a daunting prospect for Adele. She worried that few people would buy tickets to her shows and that she would be singing to empty seats. She also feared performing in front of people who had no idea what her music sounded like or what the lyrics of her songs were. And she wasn't used to being away from home for long periods of time. She knew she'd miss her friends and family.

But she was determined to succeed in the United States, and that meant putting in some time there. Her first U.S. gig was at Joe's Pub in New York City. This small, intimate nightclub is known for bringing in an exciting range of talented artists from around the world to perform live. The sound quality in the club is high. Other British performers—including Amy Winehouse—had made their U.S. debuts there. New

A small club: Adele played her first show in the United States at Joe's Pub in New York City *(a club DJ at work above)*.

Yorkers were excited about the buzz surrounding Adele's show. They knew she was an exciting new talent. Adele herself was nervous as she took the stage on May 17, 2008. A head cold made it harder for her to control her voice and added to her stress.

She opened her set with "Daydreamer." For some songs, she accompanied herself on guitar. On others, a pianist provided the musical support. In typical Adele fashion, she wore a casual, comfortable outfit—black pants and a bulky, knit sweater. Afterward, one reviewer noted that Adele closed her eyes through much of the performance—likely as a way to calm her nerves. But between songs, she seemed fairly comfortable. Adele has always been known for her conversational banter with the audience between songs, and this night was no different. She charmed the crowd with her British working-class accent and with amusing stories. She finished up a ten-song set with "Hometown Glory."

The show was a hit with the audience. One music blogger wrote: "I just can't stop thinking about how amazing her voice is. She said she had a bad cold, but you could have fooled me. Obviously, she takes guidance from the founding singers of soul and jazz, Etta James, Ella Fitzgerald and Sarah Vaughn. When you think about, the music and that style of singing is timeless. Adele's voice is very much in the now, as well as something you can think of as classic."

Adele's U.S. tour wasn't just about playing small venues. A big part of it was doing media promotion. Adele was booked on a wide range of TV and radio programs, including *Late Night with David Letterman* and the *Today Show*. She later recalled a moment of panic while performing on Letterman. Midway through her song, she forgot whether the show was live or prerecorded. She said that when she watched it afterward, she could see the confusion on her face.

A little confusion wasn't her biggest problem, however. Adele wasn't happy on tour in the United States. She was terribly homesick and lonesome. Many of the questions she faced from interviewers focused on her appearance. They talked about her weight and her less-than-glamorous style of dress. Adele wasn't ashamed of who she was, but she was tired of having to answer for it. She was relieved when the U.S. leg of her tour was finally over in late June.

A Crisis and a Stroke of Luck

Adele was happy to return home. She was tired of promoting her album and felt as if she was missing out on life. She was dealing with a troubled romantic relationship and with a drinking problem. She just didn't feel like touring. So she canceled some future dates in the United States and took a break—a period she later referred to as her early-life crisis.

Late night: Adele arrives for her appearance on the *Late Show with David Letterman* in July 2008.

"I was drinking far too much and that was kind of the basis of my relationship with this boy," she later confessed. "I couldn't bear to be without him, so I was like, 'Well, OK, I'll just cancel my stuff then. . . .' I was desperately unhappy."

While Adele was struggling to get her personal life in order, *19* was finally released in the United States on June 10, 2008. It was a critical success. *Billboard* magazine raved about the album. "While pop-friendly in melody, there's an old-soul weariness that pervades Adele's sweet, husky vocals. . . . Adele truly has potential to become among the most respected and inspiring international artists of her generation."

Musical Influence: Mary J. Blige

Mary J. Blige, born January 11, 1971, in the Bronx, New York, is one of the most influential women in pop music. She is a successful vocalist, producer, actress, and businesswoman. Her mix of R & B, rap, pop, and gospel have inspired countless artists, including Adele, who love Blige's raw and gritty sound.

Blige's career started in 1992 with her debut album release, *What's the 411?* She was an overnight star, powered by singles such as "Real Love" and "You Remind Me." She built on that success two years later with *My Life*, widely regarded as her best album.

Blige continued to release hit af-ter hit throughout the 1990s and the early 2000s. But she didn't just sing. She also became a successful record producer. In 2004 she started her own label, Matriarch Records. The label released the soundtrack to the film *Precious* (2009), as well as several offerings from Blige herself. Six years later, she launched her own fragrance, called My Life. She also acted on several TV shows and films, including 2009's *I Can Do Bad All By Myself* and 2012's *Rock of Ages*.

Blige remains a force in the music industry, especially in R & B. In 2010 the TV network VH1 listed her among the top 100 recording artists of all time.

Queen of Hip-Hop Soul: Mary J. Blige performs at the Grammy Awards ceremony in 2007. She took home three awards that year, for best R & B song, best R & B album, and best female R & B Vocal Performance.

But despite the critical acclaim, album sales were lagging in the United States. To boost sales, Adele needed to promote herself more. So she ended her break and headed back to the United States to get back to work. A producer on the popular late-night comedy show *Saturday Night Live* (*SNL*) had seen her perform in New York and had loved her. The producer booked Adele to sing on the October 18, 2008, episode of *SNL*. It was a great opportunity to reach a large audience.

As it happened, being booked for this particular episode of *SNL* was a huge stroke of luck for Adele. It came at a time when voters in the United States were just a few weeks out from electing a new president. The contest was exciting. Democratic candidate Barack Obama was battling for votes against Republican candidate John McCain. If elected, Obama would be the nation's first African American president. Americans were following the contest closely. On August 29, 2008, McCain announced his choice of running mate—Alaska governor Sarah Palin. It was a controversial decision. Many Republicans loved Palin for her plainspoken ways and conservative politics. They were excited to have a woman as the party's first-ever vice-presidential pick. Meanwhile, many other Americans mocked her. They worried that she did not have the experience and wisdom to serve as the nation's vice president. Palin was a lightning rod, and it seemed everyone was interested in her one way or the other. Two weeks after

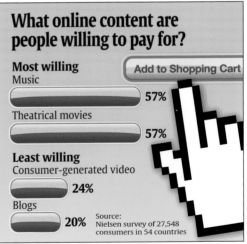

USA TODAY Snapshots®

What online content are people willing to pay for?

Most willing
Music
57%
Add to Shopping Cart

Theatrical movies
57%

Least willing
Consumer-generated video
24%

Blogs
20%

Source: Nielsen survey of 27,548 consumers in 54 countries

By Anne R. Carey and Alejandro Gonzalez, USA TODAY, 2010

SNL: Adele sang "Chasing Pavements" on *Saturday Night Live* on October 18, 2008. The show was the third-highest-rated program of the week because vice-presidential candidate Sarah Palin was a guest that night.

McCain announced his decision, comedian Tina Fey impersonated Palin brilliantly on *SNL*. Viewers ate it up.

Amid the frenzy, Palin herself agreed to appear on the show in mid-October—and she would share the limelight with Adele. With all eyes on Palin, interest in *SNL* skyrocketed. An estimated 17 million viewers tuned in to see how the candidate would handle the comedy show. It was *SNL*'s highest-rated show in more than a decade. Many of those viewers were still tuned in when Adele took the stage to perform

Adele performed with the orchestral group Wired Strings. She wore a simple black dress and sweater, appearing calm and in control as she belted out "Chasing Pavements." She was expressive and looked even a bit emotional. She finished the song with a big note. As the music faded, Adele backed away from the microphone and gave a little bow and a little grin to the audience. In an instant, all the confidence she'd had while singing seemed to melt away. She suddenly

IN F⊕CUS

Oops

Some stars seem as if they never screw up. Adele isn't one of them. She has had some famous blunders over the years. For example, when she first saw Republican vice-presidential candidate Sarah Palin backstage at *SNL* in 2008, she confused her with Tina Fey. She even ran up to Palin, shouting Tina's name.

On another occasion, Adele got a phone call from music legend Elton John. She didn't believe it was really Elton so she hung up! While shooting a video in Los Angeles in 2010, Adele almost ran over rapper Sean Combs (P Diddy) with a golf cart. "I almost, almost killed him!" she later said. And on New Year's Eve 2008, she was out in a designer outfit and high heels (she usually wears flats). She lost her balance, fell down a hill, and landed in dog poop!

Politics: In September 2008, Alaska governor Sarah Palin *(above)* accepted the nomination to run as John McCain's vice-presidential running mate. On the *SNL* set, Adele confused her with comedian Tina Fey.

appeared shy and nervous, even wringing her hands as she waited for the show to cut to commercial.

Later, Adele took the stage for a second song, "Cold Shoulder." It was more of the same. She offered smooth, controlled vocals and an almost laid-back appearance. Adele was into the song, grooving, moving her hands and even her body. She finished up strong, gave the audience a smile and a sheepish thumbs-up.

The *SNL* exposure paid off for Adele right away. Impressed by Adele's voice, fans hurried to their computers to download *19*. Overnight, Adele was at the top of the U.S. download charts. And suddenly, U.S. fans were behind Adele, just as the critics had been months before.

In Demand

As a result of the *SNL* appearance, U.S. sales of Adele's *19* soared. Her album peaked at number 4 on the U.S. charts. Her songs, especially "Chasing Pavements," were all over pop radio stations in the United States. At this point, Adele returned home briefly. She had been living with her mother. But when she returned to England, she moved into her own apartment in the popular London neighborhood Notting Hill. (She lived there only about a year before moving back in with her mom.) She knew that with her popularity high in the United States, it was time to get back to North America to promote herself. So in early 2009, she headed back to the United States.

New digs: Adele lived briefly in London's fashionable Notting Hill neighborhood. The area is known for its attractive townhouses *(above)*, high-end shopping, and restaurants.

February 9, 2012

Adele's Deeply Personal Style Rolls On

<u>From the Pages of</u>
<u>USA TODAY</u>

She'll sing. She'll waltz away with an armload of hardware. She'll cap a year of astonishing success in a spotlight warmed by the esteem and gratitude of a beleaguered industry buoyed by her global takeover.

See it unfurl on "The Adele Show," officially known as the 54th annual Grammy Awards, Sunday night, when the 23-year-old London-born singer is likely to pick up trophies for all six categories she's nominated in, including best album for *21* and best record and song for "Rolling in the Deep."

Praise from her peers

Adele couldn't get there without enticing all ages and tastes, from consumers who rarely buy CDs to every stripe of [music lover]. And lots of singers.

Country/pop singer LeAnn Rimes, who has earned raves for her live cover of Adele's "Someone Like You," has been a fan from the start. "'Chasing Pavements,' both the song and the unique video, is what first caught my attention," she says. "I found her writing fresh, and for someone who was so young, her lyrics were powerful. I fell in love with the whole *19* record. I felt like I was listening to a young girl who had lived three lifetimes already. Her delivery of a song comes from the soul. You can't teach that; it's a gift of very few."

As for *21*'s themes of love and loss, "Who in this world can't relate to those emotions?" she says. "Adele doesn't just sing; she changes your life, makes you feel like you're not alone, almost like she wrote and sang each song for you and you only."

Dave Grohl of the Foo Fighters, up for six Grammys, told USA TODAY last year: "People are blown away that Adele is selling so many records. I'm not. That record is great! She's got a beautiful voice, and people are shocked when they hear actual talent. Music should be more than ad placement, more than synthesized looping of a voice that's been Auto-Tuned and an image made to look like a superhero or supermodel."

Britney Spears, Lady Gaga, Kanye West and Matthew Morrison have expressed admiration. Beyoncé told the singer, "When I listen to you, I feel like I'm listening to God."

Christina Aguilera posted a photo of herself with Adele on Twitter and gushed, "'Someone Like You' is my favorite! ... love u Adele."

—Edna Gunderson

By this time, Adele was a hot ticket. She wouldn't be limited to small, intimate venues anymore. Instead, she played larger, more well-known venues such as the 9:30 Club in Washington, D.C., and the Warfield in San Francisco, California. Her growing fame was hard for her to grasp at first. "The whole year's been a bit random," she said. "It's a bit bizarre, but I wouldn't change anything for the world.... It's all gone so fast that it's impossible to notice everything that's happened, let alone take it all in."

Grammy Dreams

The buzz around Adele and *19* kept growing. Her star was rising fast, and rumors swirled that she might be up for a Grammy Award. In late 2008, she got the news she'd been waiting for. She hadn't been nominated for one Grammy. She'd been nominated for *four*! The categories were Best New Artist; Record of the Year; Song of the Year; and Best Pop Performance, Female. (The final three nominations were all for "Chasing Pavements.")

In an interview with a British reporter shortly after the

IN F⬤CUS

Scared Off

Adele has followed the lead of legendary British rockers the Rolling Stones and the Beatles. Like them, she displays her awards on a shelf in her bathroom. She told an interviewer that one evening, a date came to her house. She assumed that her date knew who she was, but she was wrong. He came out of the bathroom wondering who the heck she was. Apparently the revelation of her fame scared him, Adele said, because she never saw him again!

announcement, Adele made a comment that some people took badly. She said, "A Grammy is like an Oscar. You win an Oscar when you give the performance of your life. I hope this isn't the performance of my life."

Some people took this the wrong way. They thought Adele was saying that she didn't want to win a Grammy. Some reporters accused her of being ungrateful. But Adele clarified herself—she *did* want to win. She just didn't want her first album to be the peak of her career. With this explanation, the controversy quickly went away.

Not long before the Grammy ceremony, Adele agreed to do a photo shoot for *Vogue* magazine. *Vogue* editor-in-chief Anna Wintour—a big name in the fashion world—called Adele into her office. Wintour knew that stars at the Grammys are scrutinized almost as much for their

Designs: Adele *(right)* worked with U.S. fashion designer Barbara Tfank *(left)* to choose an elegant outfit for the 2009 Grammy Awards. Tfank's clients have included actress Uma Thurman and First Lady Michelle Obama.

The editor: Anna Wintour *(above)* is the highly influential editor of *Vogue* magazine. Here she arrives at a fashion show in Paris in 2012.

fashion as for their music. She wanted to help Adele look her best at the Grammys. So she asked famous designer Barbara Tfank to help Adele pick an outfit. Tfank was glad to help (and has, in fact, continued to help Adele with her fashion choices ever since). Tfank recognized that full-figured stars such as Adele would help promote the place of curvaceous women in modern fashion. So she helped Adele pick out a simple yet flattering black satin dress with a chartreuse (yellow-green) coat for contrast. She also helped Adele pick out a pair of black heels. Adele liked the look, which she has kept. Her

The prize: Adele holds the two Grammys she won in February 2009. At the ceremony, she sang "Chasing Pavements" and was joined toward the end of the song by country singer Jennifer Nettles of Sugarland.

only complaint was that the heels made her feet hurt. She ended up walking around much of the night of the ceremony in bare feet!

Aching feet was probably the only sore spot Adele faced on the night of the awards—February 8, 2009. She won two of the four Grammys for which she had been nominated—Best Pop Performance, Female and Best New Artist. She was humble and grateful onstage, giving out her thank-yous and heaping praise on the artists she had beaten. She finished out her night with a tear-filled call home to her mother. Penny was thrilled for her daughter. But Adele didn't get only praise from her mother. Penny also scolded her daughter for chewing gum while accepting her Best New Artist award!

The big 2-1: Adele celebrated her twenty-first birthday in 2009 while performing in New York. Here she admires the birthday cake that was wheeled onstage just for her.

Building on Success

■■■■

With two Grammys under her belt, Adele was a bigger star than ever in the United States. She was ready to make the most out of her quick rise to fame. So her management team booked another short U.S. tour for Adele in March 2009. Meanwhile, in the United Kingdom, she released another single, her cover of Bob Dylan's "Make You Feel My Love." Adele's version reached number 4 on the UK charts. Other awards were pouring in as well, including three BRIT awards for Best British Female, Best British Breakthrough, and Best British Single (for "Chasing Pavements").

Another Heartbreak

Adele's second U.S. tour in 2009 was short, and it was full of highlights. On her twenty-first birthday, she was in New York to perform at the Roseland Ballroom. Her mom surprised her by wheeling out a big birthday cake and having balloons drop from the ceiling. Adele appeared delighted as the audience sang "Happy Birthday." She returned the love by throwing handfuls of candy she'd bought earlier that day into the crowd.

One of the high points for Adele on the tour was to be a performance with her idol Etta James at the Hollywood Bowl in Los Angeles. James canceled at the last minute because of illness. Adele went ahead with the show, performing without the soul legend.

Outdoor performance: The Hollywood Bowl in Los Angeles, California, is the largest natural outdoor amphitheater in the United States. Adele performed there in June 2009.

IN FOCUS

Stick with the Singing

In May 2009, Adele made her debut as an actor on the popular TV show *Ugly Betty*. She played herself and sang a song at a wedding. But she assures her fans that she has no interest in an acting career.

"I cannot watch it," she said of her performance. "I play myself, but I was so sort of uncomfortable that I sound like an American putting on an English accent. . . . I am the worst actress of all time. I'm like a . . . cardboard box! I'm awful. No, I have absolutely no intention of going into acting or making perfumes. I am a singer. I will stick to what I am good at and not spread myself thin and become mediocre at everything I do."

TV time: America Ferrera *(above)* is the title character of the television show *Ugly Betty*. Adele made a guest appearance on the show in 2009, singing "Right as Rain" from her album *19*.

At about the same time, another romantic relationship was ending for Adele. She declined to name the man with whom she had been involved. She said that he wasn't a celebrity, so it didn't matter. (A 2012 report said it was celebrity photographer Alex Sturrock. Adele never confirmed his identity.) She said that she had been completely in love.

"He was my soul mate," Adele confessed. "We had everything. On every level, we were totally right. We'd finish each other's sentences and he could just pick up how I was feeling by the look in my eye, down to a T. . . . And I think that's rare when you find the full circle in one person, and I think that's what I'll always be looking for in other men."

But for reasons Adele skirted, the relationship had ended. Adele was left feeling hurt, alone . . . and looking to write music to ease her pain. It was time to record another album. Just as *19* had been about one relationship, so too would the next album.

Rolling

Even before the relationship was over, Adele had been in the studio to record a new album. Her intent had been to release a more upbeat album—a mood that reflected her emotional state at the time. But she hadn't been pleased with the music. So after the breakup, she tried again with a freshly written batch of deeply personal songs. The music was filled with the hurt and anger she was feeling.

Adele worked with a wide range of producers—and recorded in eleven different studios—as she wrote and recorded her next album. She had been exposed to U.S. country music during her American tours in 2008. She used country as a major influence on the sound of her new album. It would have a richer sound and be more produced (cleaned up and refined) than *19* had been. The country sound is most prominent on the album's fourth track, "Don't You Remember," in which Adele explores her own shortcomings in the failed relationship. The song was a late addition to the album. Adele says that she added it because she realized that she was being very harsh toward someone she had loved. She wanted to say that she understood that she had been partly responsible for the breakup as well.

Musical Influence: Lauryn Hill

Ask Adele who her favorite artist is and she's likely to reply: Lauryn Hill. Adele's mother introduced her daughter to the American singer-songwriter. Both loved her passion and brilliant songwriting.

Hill was born May 26, 1975, in South Orange, New Jersey. She joined the Haitian American hip-hop group the Fugees in 1994. The band's second album, *The Score* (1996), launched their mainstream success. The album featured a mix of original songs and unique covers. The album's breakout hit was "Killing Me Softly with His Song," a cover of a song made famous in 1973 by Roberta Flack. The album scored two Grammy Awards.

Hill launched her solo career in 1997 with the release of her album *The Miseducation of Lauryn Hill*. Hill brought in a list of stars to perform with her, including Mary J. Blige, Carlos Santana, and John Legend. The album was a huge hit, and it is an album that Adele has listed as her favorite of all time. The album earned Hill a record ten Grammy nominations in 1999. Out of the ten, she won five.

But Hill didn't enjoy her fame.

She quickly disappeared from the music scene—by her own choice. She returned in 2004 for a Fugees reunion and is reportedly working on a new solo album.

The first: At the Grammy Awards in 1999, Lauryn Hill *(above)* won five of the ten awards for which she had been nominated. She was the first female to ever be nominated ten times in one year.

The first song she worked on—just hours after the breakup—was "Rolling in the Deep." She later explained the meaning of the song's title in an interview with *Rolling Stone*. "[The title is an] adaptation of a kind of slang . . . called 'roll deep,' which means to always have someone that has your back [is looking out for you]," she said. "I thought that's what I was always going to have, and it ended up not being the case."

The song drips with anger. In the song, Adele tells her lost love that as a couple, they could have had it all, but that he threw it away. Unlike the stripped-down sound of the songs on *19*, "Rolling in the Deep" includes a rich background soundtrack, including a piano, drums, a guitar, and chanting background singers. Adele's voice never gets lost in the music, however. She recorded the song in a single take. She later recorded another, more polished version. But she and her producers agreed that it didn't match the raw emotion of the original. They liked the rougher version of the song, so that's what they kept.

The song was released in November 2010—two months before the album—to massive success, both among fans and critics. It reached number 1 on the *Billboard* Hot 100—Adele's first number 1 song in the United States—and stayed there for seven weeks. A reviewer for the British newspaper the *Sun* wrote, "[Adele's] potential is frightening. The single is an epic, foot-stomper of a pop anthem with thumping piano and a vocal you would expect from a veteran of 20 years on the road. I can't wait for the album."

21

Fans couldn't wait either. "Rolling in the Deep" had set a new standard for Adele. Everyone wanted to know whether the new album could live up to the song's power and emotional impact. Adele even considered titling the album *Rolling in the Deep*. Instead, she decided to continue the theme she had started with *19*. Since she was twenty-one years old during the recording of the new album, that's the title she gave it—*21*.

The album was released in January 2011 and immediately took the top spot on the charts in the United Kingdom and the United States.

In addition, the release of *21* gave a boost to *19*. The album had fallen off the charts, but it suddenly reappeared at number 4. Fans and critics gave *21* a warm reception. It offers one powerhouse song after another, from the biting "Rumour Has It" and the softly vulnerable "Turning Tables" to the grand power ballad "Set Fire to the Rain." The album comes full circle with the final track, "Someone Like You." In this song, Adele seems to have made peace with the breakup and wishes her ex-boyfriend happiness.

Adele explained the change of tone. "If I don't write a song like this ["Someone Like You"], I'm just

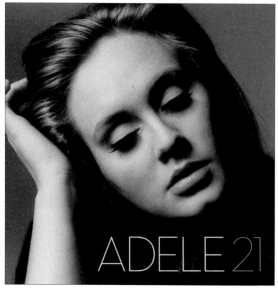

New tunes: Adele's second album, *21*, was released in January 2011. Since then it has sold more than 20 million copies.

USA TODAY Snapshots®

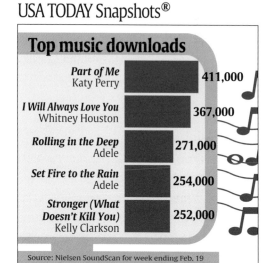

Top music downloads

Song	Downloads
Part of Me — Katy Perry	411,000
I Will Always Love You — Whitney Houston	367,000
Rolling in the Deep — Adele	271,000
Set Fire to the Rain — Adele	254,000
Stronger (What Doesn't Kill You) — Kelly Clarkson	252,000

Source: Nielsen SoundScan for week ending Feb. 19

By Steve Jones and Veronica Bravo, USA TODAY, February 2012

USA TODAY

Life

SECTION D

LIFE.USATODAY.COM

February 18, 2011

With *21*, British singer Adele opens her heart to the world

<u>From the Pages of</u>
<u>USA TODAY</u>

There are singer/songwriters who scour the world around them for inspiration, and then there is Adele.

The 22-year-old's new album, *21*, out Tuesday, is "all about one guy"—an ex-boyfriend, of course. The title refers to Adele's age "at the time I was right in the thick of" crafting the tunes. The same is true of her self-titled debut, 2008's *19*, which was also informed entirely by a single relationship.

"It's the only thing that fascinates me," Adele says, with characteristic matter-of-factness. "I can't write about other people's relationships; I'm not passionate about them. I could write about my mum, but she'd be mortified."

The formula seems to work for her. *19* catapulted Adele to stardom, first in her native UK and then here, where she collected Grammy Awards for best new artist and female pop vocal. Her resonant voice and retro-soulful style earned positive comparisons with other British songbirds such as Amy Winehouse and Duffy.

21 has already entered the charts at No. 1 in a number of countries across the Atlantic, and remained there for three weeks in England. Its first single, "Rolling in the Deep," currently sits atop USA TODAY's adult-alternative airplay chart.

The new album, which features collaborations with noted writer/producers such

going to end up becoming a bitter old woman forever. It was about putting us at peace and coming to terms with the fact that, though I'd met the love of my life, it was just bad timing."

In her own life at this time, Adele was trying to move on with her romantic life. She even signed up for an online dating service. She said that writing the album helped her deal with her emotions. "After I

as Rick Rubin and Ryan Tedder, is a more distinctive work than its predecessor, says *Rolling Stone* deputy managing editor Nathan Brackett. "She took what was good about her first record, that she's such a convincing singer, and really built on that," he says. "I hear more emotion now."

That may be because Adele was, and still is, more emotional about the subject matter. "It was my first grown-up relationship," she says of the union charted on *21*. She won't identify her muse, except to say that she met him while promoting *19*. "When you do what I do for a living, you're put in a sort of bubble, and he burst mine, which was amazing. Everything we did, we did together. Everything I did, I did for him."

Adele's previous beau [boyfriend], the one who inspired *19*, "cheated on me, and that's why we broke up. But this time, we just stopped loving each other, which was devastating. I thought I was dying. Sometimes I still can't imagine living the rest of my life without him."

A year and a half later, Adele is sufficiently recovered to have enjoyed a brief winter fling. ("We broke up yesterday," she announces casually.) But as she prepares to tour Europe and then North America, where she'll begin shows May 12 in Washington, D.C., she admits to some reluctance about taking her new songs on the road.

"I love touring," she says. "But even with the first record, which wasn't as draining as this one was, I used to get really emotional after performing certain songs. And really embarrassed, too—that here I was, two and a half years later, still singing about this guy. . . ."

Adele leans back and cackles, a deep, full-throated laugh that, like her singing, belies her tender age and reinforces her unself-conscious pluck [courage].

"I always have to step away from the songs anyway," she says. "They belong to the people who listen to them. And seeing people respond to them the way I respond to other artists—that takes my breath away."

—Elysa Gardner

wrote it, I felt more at peace," she said. "It set me free. I'm wiser in my songs. My words are always what I can never say. I'm never gonna write a song like ["Someone Like You"] again. I think that's the song I'll be known for."

The critical response to the album was almost unanimously positive. Barry Walters of the American music magazine *Spin* wrote,

Squashing the Rumors

As Adele's fame grew, she became more and more frustrated with rumors about her life. In fact, this frustration inspired her song "Rumour Has It." She got to a point where she didn't trust many of the people close to her to respect her privacy. To test their loyalty, she would make up things to tell different people in her life. Then she would sit back and wait to see what came up in the tabloid newspapers. If something she had told to only one person showed up, she knew which person had shared the information. This method told her whom she could trust and whom she couldn't trust.

"[Adele] wails harder and writes bolder, piling on the dramatic production flourishes to suggest a lover's apocalypse." Simon Harper of the British music magazine *Clash* commented on Adele's apparent growth since the release of *19*. "In the two years between the titles of Adele's debut and this, her second album, she's clearly seen the world. Where *19* marked the turbulent swan song [end] to a teenage life, *21* introduces the realities of adult life, where grown-up responsibilities collide with heartache and emotional scars run deep."

A Problem Emerges

Everything seemed to be going well for Adele. But a problem was growing. In January 2011, she was doing a promotional appearance on a French radio station in Paris. Suddenly, her voice gave out on her.

"I've been singing properly every day since I was about fifteen or sixteen," she explained later to *Vogue*. "I have never had any problems with my voice, ever. I've had a sore throat here and there, had a cold and sung through it, but that day it just went while I was onstage in

Paris during a radio show. It was literally like someone had pulled a curtain over it."

Adele saw a doctor and was diagnosed with laryngitis. This condition is the inflammation of the larynx, or voice box, which leads to a husky voice or to losing the voice temporarily. Adele needed to do just one thing, according to the doctor—rest her voice. So Adele stayed quiet for nine days. She stopped smoking and quit drinking alcohol and caffeine. She let her voice rest thoroughly so she would be ready for her upcoming world tour to support *21*.

The Performance of a Lifetime

Adele's voice was back at full strength by mid-February for the BRIT Awards. When she had been honored there two years before, she hadn't really felt that she belonged. That was no longer true. This time, she knew, she'd earned her spot there. People were tuning into the program just to see the soul sensation in action.

Large audience: The BRIT Awards are the British equivalent of the U.S. Grammys. Top celebrities attend the event, which is watched by millions of television viewers each year.

About sixteen thousand people attended the ceremony in London. An estimated six million more viewers watched on TV. The show featured some of the best-selling acts in Britain. Many of the acts featured wild stage shows, elaborate dance routines, and thrilling props. But Adele wanted none of that. She wanted people focusing on nothing but the music.

Adele has always felt nervous before performances. The anxiety of stage fright is common among performers. That night her fears were heightened. She was singing for a massive audience, including many of her peers. Her experience with laryngitis didn't help calm her nerves either. But her voice was ready. A spotlight revealed her standing on the stage next to a piano. With her hair pulled into a neat bun, she wore an elegant beaded black dress. She started to sing "Someone Like You," which had been released only a few weeks before, and immediately pulled everyone in. The power in her voice built slowly, bigger and bigger, and the audience cheered in anticipation as she approached

Emotional: Adele gave a powerful performance of her song "Someone Like You" at the 2011 BRIT Awards in London.

the chorus. A rain of glitter—her lone stage gimmick—fell on her as she belted out the emotional conclusion to the song. She was visibly emotional as she sang, appearing to fight back tears. As the final note rang out, the audience gave her a standing ovation, and tears finally spilled down her face. She later admitted that she imagined her ex-boyfriend watching the performance on TV, knowing that she was singing about him.

It was an amazingly powerful moment for many in attendance and watching on TV. The video clip posted to YouTube would later get millions of views. Even host James Corden appeared moved by it. "Wow," he said. "Wasn't that amazing? You can have all the dancers, the pyrotechnics [fireworks], laser shows you want, but if you sound like that, all you need is a piano. Incredible."

Adele was everywhere. It seemed like nothing could stop her.

Shoots: Adele poses for a publicity shot in February 2011 to promote her new album *21*. Shortly after the album's release, she went on tour.

Silenced

In early 2011, Adele set off on a tour, called Adele Live, to promote her new album. She scheduled shows all around Europe and North America, beginning in March. The tour kicked off in Europe, to rave reviews. It was typical Adele—not a lot of moving around onstage but plenty of banter between songs. Those looking for loud stage shows would have left disappointed. Adele's shows offer a more subdued atmosphere. Adele was backed by just a piano for some songs and a five-piece band for others. She sang mostly songs from *21*, though she opened each show with "Hometown Glory." She closed each show with an encore, consisting of "Rolling in the Deep" and "Someone Like You."

Adele took a few days off after the European leg of the tour, which included stops from Norway to Spain to Italy. She proudly declared that the time off was for partying. But it was also time to gear up for the next leg of the tour. This would include a grueling twenty shows in the United States and Canada.

Stirring Up Controversy

Adele didn't stay out of the news during her break before the North American tour. During an interview, she made some controversial comments about paying taxes. "I'm mortified to have to pay 50 percent [in taxes]," she said. She went on to complain about the quality of public transportation and public schools [in Britain]. She then added, "When I got my tax bill in, I was ready to go buy a gun and randomly open fire."

Fans: Adele has faced criticism for some of her public remarks, but her fans are forgiving. Here she signs autographs before a concert in Dublin, Ireland, in April 2011.

For many people, these were very inflammatory statements. Most people understood that the part about buying a gun was not to be taken seriously, even though it was in poor taste. But many fans were offended by Adele complaining about money. She was bringing in millions—most of it coming from her hardworking fans, who shelled out cash for albums and concert tickets. Some fans and reporters pointed out that Adele had gotten her start in music in a state-funded school, which wouldn't have existed without tax revenue. Others suggested

IN F◉CUS

Musical Influence: The Cure

Although Adele was too young to remember it, the Cure was the first act she ever saw live. The band was a favorite of her mother's, however, and she grew up listening to them. On her album *21*, Adele covered their hit "Lovesong."

The Cure formed in England in 1976 and has remained active ever since. The Cure started out as a new-wave rock band, experimenting with new sounds, such as punk. The band's lineup has changed a lot over the years, but vocalist Robert Smith has been there all along. The band struggled during the early 1980s and considered breaking up. But Smith took the group in a more pop-friendly direction, following the increased popularity of gothic rock. The band's breakout album came in 1989 with *Disintegration*. The album features several hit singles, including "Fascination Street" and "Lullaby." But it was "Lovesong" that really launched the band's popularity. "Lovesong" reached number 2 on the *Billboard* chart in 1989 and got massive play on the radio and on MTV.

The band's popularity has diminished since *Disintegration*. Their thirteenth studio album, *4:13 Dream* (2008), peaked at number 16 on the U.S. charts. Many music critics credit the Cure for being an important influence in bringing alternative rock into the mainstream.

that she leave England if she didn't like paying her share. The reactions were not all negative, however. Some of Britain's antitax groups stood up to support her. These groups feel that the nation's tax rates are too high and place too heavy a burden on citizens.

Warning Signs

As the controversy simmered, Adele was headed to North America for her sold-out Adele Live tour. It started on May 12 in Washington, D.C. The tour included both live shows and plenty of promotional appearances. Adele seemed to be soaking it in. She happily posed for pictures with fans, signed autographs when spotted on the street, and seemed upbeat during interviews. Over the next two weeks, she did nine more shows. The tour was supposed to continue through late June. But trouble was brewing.

Vocals: Adele's vocal problems followed her to the United States for her 2011 tour. Here she performs in May 2011 in Boston, Massachusetts, to a sold-out house. Less than one month later, she had to cancel the rest of her show dates.

For months, Adele had been dealing with on-again, off-again laryngitis. And her voice troubles were back. The tour pulled into Minneapolis, Minnesota, on May 26. As always, the work of a performance starts long before the actual showtime. In Minneapolis Adele was onstage doing a sound check (a check of audio equipment to determine sound levels for the show). After singing only a few notes for the sound check, she stopped. Her voice was hurting. She couldn't continue.

"We went in to do the sound check and she started singing and the notes just weren't there," said guitarist Tim Van Der Kuil. "It was very tough on her and she was really upset."

Adele saw a throat specialist in Minneapolis, who diagnosed her with severe laryngitis. She had to cancel the show just hours before it started. The doctor told Adele that she needed to rest her voice. But Adele wasn't willing to call off the entire tour. She had a concert scheduled in Denver, Colorado, two days later, and she intended to perform.

Adele pushed herself and went onstage for the Denver show. She got through it, but her voice wasn't completely there. Still, the tour pressed on to Salt Lake City, Utah. Once again, Adele took the stage for a sound check. But this time, she realized that she just couldn't go on. She posted a note on her blog apologizing to fans. "I hate to cancel, especially at such short notice," she wrote. "I am truly devastated. I'm here in the city and I tried to do the sound check at the venue. But if I push through it tonight, it will take me longer to get better. Please forgive me."

Adele decided to give her voice a week of rest. She hoped that would be enough to allow her to resume the tour. During that time, she saw another specialist. And she heard the same advice: rest. So she did the only thing she could. She canceled the rest of the North American tour.

A Brief Return

Adele returned to London to rest. But her voice wasn't healing as quickly as she had hoped it would. She saw more doctors. One of them suspected that Adele's vocal problem wasn't simply laryngitis. He thought that she might have a hemorrhage (burst blood vessel) in her throat. The suggested remedy was the same, however: more rest.

Adele took more time off. She didn't sing at all and spoke as little as possible. At first, it seemed that her voice was healing. She decided that she could perform at the iTunes Festival in London on July 7. The news sparked a buzz among Adele's online fans. Would she really be back? Would her voice be at full strength?

Adele left little doubt. She came to the festival and belted out a powerful set. She left the stage in happy tears. "It's like 99.9 percent better, so I'm really, really happy," she said in an interview after the show. "I thought a month ago that I would never be able to sing again. So I'm really relieved. It went great and my voice isn't hurting."

Adele was excited. The third single off of *21*, "Set Fire to the Rain," had just been released in Europe and was rocketing up the charts. The song was a true power ballad about the difficulty of letting go of a relationship. Unlike many of Adele's hits, "Set Fire to the Rain" features a fast tempo and heavy background instrumentation, including a string arrangement. This led to some mixed reviews. Some critics liked the powerful sound. Others called it overproduced, arguing that the raw, personal sound that many of

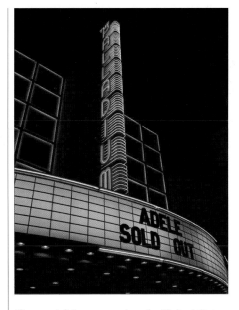

Shows: Adele returned to the United States in August 2011 to finish her tour. Her show at the Palladium theater in Hollywood, California, was sold out.

her other songs had was lacking. Regardless, the fans ate it up, and it went on to top the *Billboard* Hot 100.

Adele was eager to get back to North America to pick up where she had left off earlier in the year. Starting August 9, she did nine shows, mainly in the cities where she had canceled two months before. The sold-out shows were a big success, and the laryngitis wasn't showing any signs of return. But toward the end of the tour, Adele came down with a nagging head and chest cold. The cold got worse and worse, and soon she wasn't able to perform. She grieved her bad luck as she was forced to cancel more show dates to rest and recuperate in London.

In late September, Adele was back again, ready to get back to touring. Some members of her team suggested that she go easy on her voice. But Adele was really looking forward to the tour. One of her shows, on September 22, was at London's Royal Albert Hall.

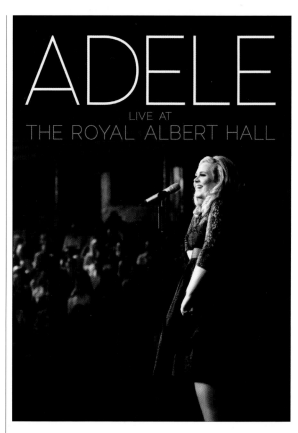

Famous hall: Adele's combination DVD-CD *Adele Live at the Royal Albert Hall (cover above)* was a huge hit in 2011. The Royal Albert Hall is a concert space in London that was built in 1871.

She was very excited to perform in this venue. The hall is famous around the world for both its elegant architecture and its long history of hosting many of the world's greatest musicians. So the show went on, full steam ahead.

Adele was at her best. She was comfortable and in full control of her voice. She hit the big notes and the softer, more subtle ones. The audience roared their approval. Adele's management decided to release a recording of the performance on a combination DVD and CD, titled *Adele Live at the Royal Albert Hall.* The package was a way to allow many more fans to experience what it was like to see Adele in concert. It went on to become the best-selling music DVD of 2011. Adele didn't know it at the time, but it was one of the last shows she would do for a long time.

The Voice Gives Out

Adele performed two more shows in Scotland, then took a short break. She was planning to resume touring in October. She felt confident about her voice and ignored pleas from some people close to her to take a long break to recover.

On October 1, one of Adele's friends was getting married. Adele agreed to sing for the couple at the ceremony. As performances go, it was about as small-scale as it gets. But the scale of the performance didn't matter. Her voice gave out entirely. Frightened, she hurried to a doctor. The news was grim. Adele had a polyp on her vocal cord, and a blood vessel near the polyp had hemorrhaged. It was a terrifying diagnosis for a singer. Her voice was her livelihood, and she feared that it might be permanently damaged. Nobody could be sure how extensive the damage was. Surgery was the only way to repair it. Adele admitted that she was scared and that she cried a lot.

Rumors flew around the Internet. Some said Adele had throat cancer. She would never sing again. Others said she was deeply depressed and suicidal.

IN FOCUS

The Vocal Cords

Adele's voice troubles came from a polyp on her vocal cords. So what exactly are the vocal cords?

When a person speaks or sings, he or she creates most of the sound with a part of the throat called the larynx—also called the voice box. The vocal cords—also known as vocal folds—are two folded membranes that stretch across the larynx. During speech, air is forced out of the larynx through the vocal cords. The cords vibrate as the air passes through, creating sound. The speed of the cords' vibration determines the tone that comes out of the speaker's mouth.

Adele's problem came when a growth called a polyp formed on the vocal cords. A vocal cord polyp is a little like a blister. It may have formed from abuse or overuse of the voice. For most people, this isn't a big problem. But singers like Adele use their voices so heavily that the polyp never gets to heal. (Adele has said she believes that her loud speaking voice, not her singing, is what damaged her vocal cords.) When her polyp hemorrhaged, surgery became the only option.

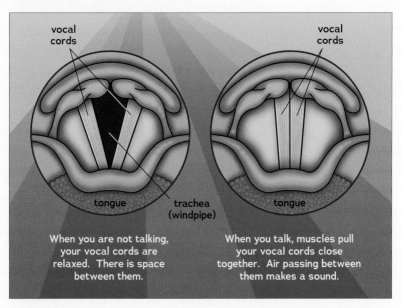

vocal cords

vocal cords

tongue

trachea (windpipe)

tongue

When you are not talking, your vocal cords are relaxed. There is space between them.

When you talk, muscles pull your vocal cords close together. Air passing between them makes a sound.

Voice box: This illustration shows the vocal cords in the larynx.

Adele was annoyed by all the false rumors. She wanted her fans to know the truth. "Singing is literally my life," she wrote in an official statement released by Columbia Records, her U.S. label. "It's my hobby, my love, my freedom and now my job. I have absolutely no choice but to recuperate properly and fully or I risk damaging my voice forever."

Under the Knife

Adele headed back to the United States. Only this time, it wasn't to perform. She had been forced to cancel the rest of her concert dates for 2011. This time, she was headed to Boston, Massachusetts, home of the Massachusetts General Hospital Voice Center. There she met with Dr. Steven Zeitels, a leader in the field of vocal cord surgery. Adele later said that she immediately trusted Zeitels, who had worked with many singers, including Stephen Tyler of the rock band Aerosmith. "When I met him I loved him," she said of Zeitels. "He made me feel safe."

Famous surgeon: Steven Zeitels is a distinguished laryngeal (larynx) surgeon from New York. He is known for developing new surgical instruments and creative new surgical procedures. Zeitels performed Adele's surgery in 2011.

February 10, 2012

Grammys will be Adele's vocal 'debut'

From the Pages of USA TODAY Adele's storybook success took a terrifying turn last fall when the British singer was diagnosed with a polyp on her vocal cord that had hemorrhaged. After laser microsurgery in November, she spent weeks recovering under orders to not speak or sing. Her return to the microphone at the Grammy Awards is seen as a glorious rebound.

"Typically, following vocal fold surgery of the type she had, she will be closely monitored by her voice team," says Milan R. Amin, director of the New York University Voice Center at NYU Langone Medical Center. "On average, patients are allowed to start singing under close guidance about six weeks after surgery. They obviously start slowly and progress under the care of a voice teacher.

"The time frame from her surgery to the Grammys seems reasonable. If all went well with the surgery and the recovery, her vocal folds should be in great shape."

Voice training to prevent a recurring problem would be wise, says Maitland Peters, voice department chair at New York's Manhattan School of Music.

"It is critically important that a vocal athlete such as Adele develops a strong technique in order to withstand the extreme stress that the vocal cords are under when performing," he says. "She needs to be extremely careful in this performance so soon after surgery to ensure that her voice remains healthy and strong for her future."

Adele seems aware of the risks. In a *60 Minutes* interview airing Sunday, she says, "If I decide to go on a 200-date world tour, it would happen again."

The toughest aspect of her recovery was enforced silence, until she found a phone app that translated her typed words into spoken words. "I found this one app where you can swear," she says.

Adele's career scare should serve "as a wake-up call to singers that the voice has to be taken care of properly," says Recording Academy president Neil Portnow.

"All of us in the industry were concerned," says Portnow, who was reassured after speaking to Adele's doctor. "He performs incredible medical miracle work on many other recording artists, and he told me that she was remarkably resilient and had done really well and that she would shine and soar. Expectations are high but they will be met."

—Edna Gunderson

Zeitels performed the surgery on November 3, 2011. He used a medical laser to remove the polyp and repair the hemorrhage. The surgery was a success. The hospital released a statement saying that Dr. Zeitels expected Adele to make a full recovery. Still, many fans worried. Would Adele really be able to come back?

Back with awards: After recuperating from her surgery, Adele was back in full force. Here she accepts an Ivor Novello Award for Music Most Performed Work at an awards ceremony in London in May 2012.

Adele Is Back

The surgery had been a success, but that didn't make life much easier for Adele. She had to be completely silent for at least three weeks. It was something that didn't come naturally to her. At first she communicated by writing on cards, but that wasn't good enough. Later, she got an app for her iPhone that would read out what she typed. And finally, she found an even better app (better, she said, because it allowed her to swear!). She also liked to use the app to communicate with fans she met while out shopping, getting coffee, and going about her everyday life.

Adele also used the time to catch her breath and reflect on everything that had happened to her. She said the time off was a blessing. It allowed her to appreciate what she had achieved. It also spurred her toward living a healthier lifestyle. She vowed to eat more healthfully and to stop smoking. Before the surgery, she had not been interested in losing weight to improve her image. But when it came to her health, she was willing to do so. She reportedly dropped more than 20 pounds (9 kilograms). The slimmer body, she said, was just a bonus. It was all about getting herself into a healthier place, both physically and emotionally.

"I think I just needed to be silenced," she said. "And when you are silent, everyone else around you is silent. So the noise in my life just stopped. It was like I was floating in the sea for three weeks. It was brilliant. It was my body telling me to fix me. I had so much time to kind of go over things and get over things, which is amazing. I think if I hadn't had my voice trouble, I would never have broached those subjects with myself. Now I just feel really at peace. And really proud of myself. I've never fully appreciated the things that I've achieved until now. In fact, my entire life has changed in the last ten weeks. I've never been so happy, and I love it.

While Adele recovered, the fourth single from *21* was released worldwide. The bluesy, jazzy "Rumour Has It" was already familiar to Adele fans. The song had sold half a million copies—mainly in the United States and the United Kingdom—even before the record label formally released it. With the release, that figure soared over the million mark. It was well received critically, though it peaked at just number 16 on *Billboard*'s Hot 100 chart.

New Voice, New Love

By mid-December, Adele's doctors gave her the go-ahead to begin rebuilding the strength in her voice.

February 9, 2012

Adele's Deeply Personal Style Rolls On

<u>From the Pages of</u>
<u>USA TODAY</u>

While little suspense surrounds the [Grammy] awards ceremony, fans and peers are eager to hear Adele in her first live performance since canceling tours in October to have throat surgery in November for a vocal cord hemorrhage.

Adele gives promise to the future. Her inevitable coronation acknowledges the increasingly rare talent that unites fans across today's fractured musical landscape.

"The songs are so powerful and accessible," says Ken Ehrlich, executive producer of the Grammy Awards. "You can be a 14-year-old girl or a 60-year-old guy and love those songs. Did the autobiographical nature have much to do with it? For a certain segment of the audience, yes. Music in recent years has become more impersonal and so much about the beat. Her songs make you stop and listen."

In the era of declining music sales, Adele is proof that a sublime talent and compelling songs can still draw the masses, says Don Was, Grammy-winning producer, musician and president of Blue Note Records.

"Don't say it's over," Was says. "If you offer people something organically soulful, they will buy CDs. She's an honest singer making real modern soul music. You don't get the sense that someone is putting it together in a computer."

Adele, her producer Paul Epworth and her label "made a great record and let people know about it," he says. "It's axiomatic [obvious] stuff. Every record should be that good. I think it's an encouraging sign, and I hope the message won't get lost: Be for real, make great records, and people will support you."

Adele got a U.S. toehold with 2008 debut *19* and its single "Chasing Pavements." The album jumped to No. 11 from No. 46 in *Billboard* after a fortuitously timed performance on *Saturday Night Live* that drew huge ratings for a Sarah Palin appearance. Her second album *21*, a mix of soulful ballads and bouncier tunes inspired by a breakup, entered *Billboard* at No. 1 after selling 352,000 copies its first week. Sales never flagged.

"Lightning in a bottle"

Now in its 19th non-consecutive week at No. 1, *21* has sold 6.39 million copies, according to Nielsen SoundScan. "Rolling" (6.18 million downloads sold), "Someone" (4.15 million) and current single "Set Fire to the Rain" (2.37 million) all peaked at No. 1 while *21* topped the album chart, the first such triple-header since 1978's *Saturday Night Fever* soundtrack.

"The way this record built and continued to sell strong through the year, it's bucking the trend," says Dave Bakula, a senior analyst at Nielsen SoundScan. "Typically, you get a nice release week, and then sales tail off. Based on what we've seen since 2004, this kind of sustainability is a very rare occurrence.

"It's a great story in artist discovery and development. This time last year, not a lot of people were talking about Adele. She wasn't a household name, and there wasn't so much pent-up demand that you could see this coming."

The tally for *21* represented 2 percent of all albums scanned in 2011, says Bakula. "People hear it, love it and have to have it," he says. "The demand was tremendous, but there wasn't an incredible media blitz like the promotion you see with Lady Gaga. It was lightning in a bottle."

How far can she go?

A few years ago, "if somebody told you that a future album would sell 5.82 million copies in a calendar year, you'd have thought they were either out of touch with sales trends or a cheerleader for the music industry," [Paul] Grein [who writes the weekly Chart Watch blog for Yahoo] says. "It will be interesting to see how far this album can go. Songs are still getting heavy airplay. Adele is certain to sweep the Grammys. Can it reach 10 million? I wouldn't bet against it."

"People hold on to this idea that iTunes and YouTube ... killed superstars, but YouTube has been a great promotional tool for artists like Adele," says [Glenn Peoples, *Billboard*'s senior editorial analyst], noting that her *Rolling* video, with 227.6 million views, ranks 18th on YouTube's top videos of all time.

Even Adele says she feels stirred by her wrenching tunes. "'Someone Like You' moves me," she said on a recent episode of the PBS series *Live From the Artists Den*. "I don't listen to my music, but if I need to cry, I will listen to that song. . . . Every time I sing a song, something else comes out a little bit more of me is devastated or gutted and disappointed."

She told *Interview* magazine last year: "It's warts and all in my songs, and I think that's why people can relate to them. I write about love, and everyone ... knows what it is like to have your heart broken."

—Edna Gunderson

It started with some simple humming. By late December, she started a little singing. She wasn't performing or belting out notes. She just sang along with music or sang softly in the shower. Among the songs she sang were "Happy Birthday" and "The Grand Old Duke of York," an English nursery rhyme set to music.

As she sang more, Adele noticed that something had changed. "[My voice] feels really smooth," she said. "It's not as husky as it used to be, but that's because I was singing with a polyp. And it's higher than it used to be. Which is a bit weird. I really thought if my voice changed an octave it would go lower. But it still sounds like me. It's really easy to sing. It's a pleasure. And I haven't felt like that for quite a while."

Meanwhile, Adele had met and fallen in love with a new man.

Love: Seated with Adele, Simon Konecki— the new love in Adele's life—attended the Grammy Awards in February 2012.

Photographers spotted her arm-in-arm with thirty-six-year-old Simon Konecki, a former investment banker. Adele had met Konecki during the summer of 2011, when she took an interest in the charity he ran, Drop4Drop. The charity's goal is to help deliver clean water to underdeveloped regions of the globe. The two started dating before Adele's vocal cord hemorrhage, and by the end of the year, it had grown serious.

"He's wonderful," Adele said of Konecki. "And he's proud of me, but he don't care about what I do or what other people think.

IN F⊕CUS

Drop4Drop

Adele met Simon Konecki after becoming involved with the charity Drop4Drop. The charity's mission is to help people in undeveloped regions of the globe get access to clean drinking water. The charity helps communities drill water wells, provides water purification kits and water filters, and improves water sanitation efforts. Drop4Drop's projects have spanned the globe, from Haiti to West Africa to India.

Water charity: This screen shot shows the home page of Drop4Drop, the charity run by Adele's boyfriend Simon Konecki.

He looks after me. I don't think I would have gotten through the recovery for my surgery if it hadn't been for him."

The relationship became public in early 2012, after the couple was spotted vacationing in Florida. Rumors soon swirled that the couple was engaged, but Adele denied it. Regardless, the couple was already beginning to plan for a future together.

The Grammys

The good news just kept coming for Adele. The Grammy nominations were announced in late 2011, and she was up for six awards, including Album of the Year for *21*. She said the news brought tears to her eyes. She believed that *21*'s run at the top of the charts was coming to an end and thought that winning a Grammy would be the perfect way to move on.

The organizers of the Grammy Awards asked Adele to perform at the ceremony as well. After some thought, Adele agreed. Fans and

Belting it out: Adele made a triumphant return to the stage after her surgery, performing "Rolling in the Deep" at the 2012 Grammy Awards ceremony.

reporters had recently questioned whether she would ever sing again. What better place to answer that question than at the biggest music awards ceremony of the year?

"For it to be my first performance in months is very exciting and of course nerve-wracking," she said in a statement. "But what a way to get back into it all."

Adele was the headliner for the show. The CBS television network

Winner: Adele gleefully accepts her 2012 Grammy for Record of the Year.

ran advertisements to tout her long anticipated, big return. The TV news magazine *60 Minutes* ran a feature on Adele and her return to the stage on the night of the awards. Adele spoke candidly about her rapid rise to fame, the health of her vocal cords, her recovery from surgery, and her stage fright.

When the time came for her to take the stage, she didn't disappoint. She looked elegant in her Giorgio Armani gown, which showed off her new, slimmer figure. She also sported a new hairstyle—shorter and blonder than she'd ever worn it before. And best of all, she belted out a confident, powerful version of "Rolling in the Deep." She had no vocal troubles at all that night, and the audience showed its enthusiasm with a standing ovation. Adele went on to win all six awards for which she had been nominated. She took home Album of the Year and Best Pop Vocal Album for *21*; Record of the Year, Song of the Year, and Best Short Form Music Video for "Rolling in the Deep"; and Best

Pop Solo Performance for "Someone Like You." Her six awards tied her with Beyoncé for the most won by a female in a single year.

During one acceptance speech, as she talked about the inspiration for *21*, Adele broke down in tears. "It's gone on to do things—I can't tell you how I feel about it. It's been a life changing year."

Adele's big night reignited fan interest in her album. Sales soared. Her singles rocketed back up to the top of the charts in the United States and the United Kingdom. In late February, she became the first female in the fifty-three-year history of the *Billboard* Hot 100 chart to have three singles in the top 10. "Set Fire to the Rain" sat at number 2. "Rolling in the Deep"—in its fifty-ninth week on the chart—climbed back to number 5. And "Someone Like You" jumped to number 7. And if that wasn't enough, she also had both of her albums in the *Billboard* 200's top 5. The album *21* sat in the top spot, while *19* jumped up to number 4—two and a half years after its release! The booming sales were a testament to Adele's ability to write music that spoke to people of all generations and backgrounds.

Staying on Top

A few weeks after the Grammys, Adele was at the 2012 BRIT Awards. She performed "Rolling in the Deep." By Adele's modest standard, it was an elaborate performance. She was bathed in spotlights and stood before a backing band, which featured a piano, drums, and three guitars, as well as backup singers. Adele delivered a great vocal, complete with a heavy dose of attitude, which even included a little snarl coming out of the first chorus. She encouraged the audience to clap along to the beat. By the end, the audience was on its feet.

Adele also won two of the three awards for which she had been nominated. As award shows often do, the televised BRIT Awards were running long. Toward the end of the ceremony, television producers were trying to hurry things along to stay close to the scheduled running time. During Adele's acceptance speech for Album of the Year, the show's host purposely cut her off.

IN FOCUS

Musical Influence: INXS

Adele lists INXS as one of her favorite bands. She's even hinted that she will cover their song, "Never Tear Us Apart," on a future album.

The band started in Australia in 1977 as the Farriss Brothers. The name came from three of the band's members—Andrew, Tim, and Jon Farriss. Their vocalist was Michael Hutchence, and other longtime members include Garry Gary Beers and Kirk Pengilly. The band changed its name to INXS (pronounced "in excess") in 1979.

INXS gained popularity in Australia in 1980. They started out playing new-wave rock. But their sound became more mainstream by the mid to late 1980s—the same period during which they achieved international fame. Their breakthrough hit was 1985's "What You Need." Later hits included "Never Tear Us Apart," "Devil Inside," and "Need You Tonight," which reached number 1 that year.

The band maintained a loyal following through the early 1990s. Then, in 1997, Hutchence died in an apparent suicide. The band stopped performing for more than a year. Then, in 2005, they were featured on the reality TV show *Rock Star: INXS*. The winner of the reality show's contest to find a lead singer for the group, J.D. Fortune, took over as lead singer. The band is no longer as popular as it once was. But it retains a loyal following and continues to tour internationally.

Aussies: The Australian rock band INXS in 1987. *From left to right:* Michael Hutchence, Kirk Pengilly, Andrew Farriss, Garry Gary Beers, Tim Farriss, and Jon Farriss.

More awards: Adele's run of success in 2012 continued with wins at that year's BRIT Awards. She shares the stage in this photo with host James Corden, who was forced to cut her acceptance speech short.

Adele, annoyed at having her speech cut short, reacted in a typical blunt fashion. She made an obscene hand gesture that was aired over live TV. The audience clearly supported her, roundly booing the host for the interruption.

"That [gesture] was for the suits [executives] at the BRIT Awards, not my fans," Adele explained. "I'm sorry if I offended anyone, but the suits offended me."

In March 2012, Adele celebrated her great run of success by buying a huge new beach home. She chose a wealthy neighborhood of Brighton, which is on England's southern coast along the English Channel. A month later, she announced her plans to make her home eco-friendly by adding solar panels to the roof. The panels capture the sun's rays and turn it into energy, helping to reduce reliance on other, less green sources of energy. Konecki helped her pick the house, and the couple made plans to move in together.

Meanwhile, Adele continued to be honored for *21*. She became a

Leaving home: Adele moved out of her house in West Sussex *(above)* to live with Simon in a beach home in Brighton.

winner for twelve separate awards at the *Billboard* Music Awards in Las Vegas, Nevada, on May 20. Her awards included Top Artist; Top Female Artist; Top Pop Album (*21*); and Top Alternative Song, "Rolling in the Deep."

Adele's achievements just kept rolling in. In May 2012, *21* topped the 9 million mark in U.S. sales. Only twenty-eight other albums in history had done this well. The album also passed Michael Jackson's album *Thriller* (1982) to become the fifth-highest-selling album in UK history. Then in June, something really unusual happened. Sixty-eight weeks after *21* was released in the United States, it was back at number 1! Music industry insiders explained that there were two main reasons *21* returned to the top spot. First, it was a slow week for new releases (*21* sold about seventy-five thousand copies that week, an unusually low number for the chart topper). Secondly, NBC had just run a special titled *Adele Live in London*. The special exposed new music fans to Adele. They loved her—and bought her album. It was an

IN F☉CUS

Rolling in the Pink

In 2012 *Time* magazine included Adele on its annual list of the most influential people in the world. She joined people from all walks of life, including businessman Warren Buffet, U.S. presidential hopeful Mitt Romney, U.S. secretary of state Hillary Rodham Clinton, and TV personality Stephen Colbert.

Grammy-award-winner Pink wrote the section about Adele. She wrote:

Adele's success renews hope in me that the world I live in has good taste—that we still occasionally come back to what's simple, and simply amazing. I can't wait to hear what she does next.

impressive accomplishment for an album almost a year and a half old.

In October Adele's fans had a new single to enjoy. A seventy-seven-piece orchestra backed her in her song "Skyfall," performed as the theme for the James Bond film of the same name. The song was met with approval from both fans and critics. Seth Abramovitch of the *Hollywood Reporter* described the song as a classic Bond theme. "Done in big, orchestral style, the mood—like the singer—is all 1960s throwback.... The lyrics, too, offer the classic Bond vibe—apocalyptically dangerous and very sexy."

The Future

Adele has been in the spotlight since she was nineteen years old. She has released two hit albums, recovered from major throat surgery, and has collected an impressive number of awards. So what does the future hold for this young superstar?

Some performers love to tour. But Adele has said that when she's on tour, she constantly feels as if she's missing out on life. She has always expressed a desire to settle down and start a family. That dream started to come true when she began dating Konecki and they bought a house together. Then, in June 2012, Adele announced some big news on her blog. She was pregnant.

"I'm delighted to announce that Simon and I are expecting our first child together," she wrote. "Obviously we're over the moon and very excited but please respect our privacy at this precious time."

Adele gave birth to a baby boy in October 2012.

Adele's fans were happy for her, but what many really wanted to know was what her plans were for her music. In an interview, Adele hinted that she might record and release another single as early as late 2012. Rumors have linked her to a theme song for the next James Bond movie. But what about another album? Adele has cautioned fans that they may have to wait a few years. "I want to evolve as an artist," she said. "There's so much music I don't know about yet. I want to go on the road with my friends who are artists. I want to go and see things as a fan again. I am a fan, but I can't remember

007: Adele's "Skyfall" is the official theme song for the latest James Bond 007 movie.

what it feels like to be a fan anymore...

"I don't want to be disposable. You're only as good as your next record. I'm not scared of losing this [fame]. I won't come out with new music until it's better than *21*.... Also, I have nothing to write about! I'd be lying. And that would go against everything I've ended up building for myself. So, yeah, I will need at least three years to write a record."

Cover girl: As Adele's star has risen, she has posed for a number of glamorous photo shoots, including this cover shot for the March 2012 issue of *Vogue*. With a successful career, a new love in her life, and a new baby, Adele's life is richly satisfying.

So what will the next album be like? With a committed relationship and a child in her life, fans can expect a much different tone from Adele. She has hinted that she wants to incorporate some bluegrass sound into a future album. Bluegrass is a type of country music, infused with elements of folk and jazz. Adele fell in love with the

IN F🔍CUS

There's an App for That?

Adele has always felt technology and the Internet play a big part in music. She was discovered on MySpace, has set records for digital downloads, and maintains a blog for her fans. In 2012 she released her own free app for cell phones and other devices that run the Android operating system. The app gives users access to the latest Adele news, concert dates, and Adele's blog. Fans can also use the app to sample Adele's music and videos, including material that hasn't been formally released. And they can communicate with one another—and occasionally with Adele herself—on fan forums.

sound while touring the United States supporting *19*.

No matter what direction her next album takes, one thing is certain. It's going to sell a lot of copies. No one can be sure if *21* was the peak of Adele's young career, or really just the start. But fans can't wait to find out.

TIMELINE

1988 Adele Laurie Blue Adkins is born on May 5 in Tottenham, an area of north London, England.

1989 Richard Russell, Tim Palmer, and Nick Halkes found XL Recordings, Adele's first recording company.

2006 A friend puts several of Adele's demo songs on MySpace.

Adele graduates from The London School for Performing Arts & Technology   (BRIT School) in May.

Adele signs with XL Recordings in September.

2007 In June Adele makes her TV debut on the British show   *Later...with Jools Holland.*

Adele's first single, "Hometown Glory," is released in Britain in October.

"Chasing Pavements" is released in the United Kingdom in December.

2008 Adele's first album, *19*, is released in Britain in January.

Adele is honored with the Critic's Choice award at the BRIT Awards in February.

Happy: Adele accepts her Critic's Choice award at the BRIT Awards in 2008.

Adele begins her first tour of the United States in May.

Big hit: Adele performs on *Saturday Night Live* in 2008.

Adele performs on *Saturday Night Live* in October.

2009   Adele wins two Grammy Awards in February.

2010   Adele writes and records her second album, *21*. The first single, "Rolling in the Deep," is released worldwide in November.

2011   The album *21* is released worldwide in January and debuts at number 1.

Adele performs an emotional version of "Someone Like You" at the BRIT Awards in February.

Adele postpones shows in the United States due to voice troubles.

Adele performs at London's Royal Albert Hall in September. The live performance is later made into a DVD.

In November Adele has surgery in the United States to remove a polyp from her vocal cords.

Late in the year, Adele begins a romantic relationship with Simon Konecki.

2012 Adele gives her first performance since her surgery at the Grammy Awards in February. She wins six Grammys.

Adele buys a home in Brighton, England, in March. She and her boyfriend plan to move in together.

In June Adele announces on her blog that she is pregnant.

Adele gives birth to a baby boy in October.

DISCOGRAPHY (U.S. RELEASE DETAILS)

19
Labels: XL Recordings, Columbia
Released: January 28, 2008

21
Labels: XL Recordings, Columbia
Released: January 19, 2011

Live at the Royal Albert Hall (DVD-CD combo)
Label: XL Recordings, Columbia, Sony Music
Released: November 25, 2011

SOURCE NOTES

7. BBC, "Grammy Glory for Returning Adele," *BBC*, February 12, 2012, http://www.bbc.co.uk/news/entertainment-arts-17007642 (May 17, 2012).

9. Chas Newkey-Burden, *Adele: The Biography* (Croydon, UK: John Blake Publishing, 2011), 2–3.

9. Jonathan Van Meter, "Adele: One and Only," *Vogue*, February 13, 2012, http://www.vogue.com/magazine/article/adele-one-and-only/#5 (June 21, 2012).

12. Newkey-Burden, *Adele*, 30.

16. Ibid., 32–33.

17. Marc Shapiro, *Adele: The Biography* (New York: St. Martin's Press, 2012), 32.

19. Joseph Patterson, "Jessie J: There Are Bad Ones That Nobody Will Ever Hear," *MTV.com*, April 20, 2011, http://www.mtv.co.uk/music/urban/267442-jessie-j-there-are-bad-ones-that-no-one-will-ever-hear (July 2, 2012).

19. Newkey-Burden, *Adele*, 39–40.

19. Ibid., 35.

20. AOL, "Adele Recalls Hearing Pink Performing Live," *Spinner.com*, n.d., http://www.spinner.com/2010/12/23/adele-defining-moments (June 29, 2012).

24. Shapiro, *Adele*, 31.

25. Newkey-Burden, *Adele*, 52.

27. Ibid., 60.

28. Shapiro, *Adele*, 41.

31. Pete Lewis, "Adele: Up Close and Personal," *B&S*, n.d., http://www.bluesandsoul.com/feature/302/the_futures_looking_rosie_for_adele/ (June 4, 2012).

35. Ibid.

36. Newkey-Burden, *Adele*, 88.

36. Sylvia Patterson, "Mad about the Girl," *Guardian* (London), January 26, 2008, http://www.guardian.co.uk/music/2008/jan/27/popandrock.britawards2008 (June 29, 2012).

37–38. Priya Elan, "Adele: *19*," *NME*, February 1, 2008, http://www.nme.com/reviews/adele/9433 (June 14, 2012).

38. Chris Long, "Adele *19* Review," *BBC*, January 18, 2008, http://www.bbc.co.uk/music/reviews/6pf9 (June 14, 2012).

40. Newkey-Burden, *Adele*, 82.

39. Ibid., 72–73.

43. Jon Bream, "Chasing Adele," *Minneapolis Star Tribune*, January 15, 2009, http://www.startribune.com/printarticle/?id=37642734 (August 26, 2012).

45. "Adele @ Joe's Pub: We're All Chasing Pavements," *MusicSnobbery,com*, March 18, 2008, http://www.musicsnobbery.com/2008/03/adele-joes-pub.html (August 14, 2012).

46. Newkey-Burden, *Adele*, 118.

46. Michael Menachem, "Chasing Pavements: Adele," June 7, 2008, http://www.billboard.biz/bbbiz/content_display/magazine/reviews/singles/e3i07a95797894eac56261967813bd2ca4c (June 17, 2012).

53. Newkey-Burden, *Adeley*, 122.

54. Shapiro, *Adele*, 86.

50. Gordon Smart, "Harry Redknapp, P Diddy and Sarah Palin . . . I've Made a Fool of Myself in Front of Them All," *Sun* (London), January 13, 2011, http://www.thesun.co.uk/sol/homepage/features/3348426/Adele-Harry-Redknapp-P-Diddy-and-Sarah-Palin-Ive-made-a-fool-of-myself-in-front-of-them-all.html (June 17, 2012).

60. Newkey-Burden, *Adele*, 160.

62. *Rolling Stone,* "Rolling in the Deep," n.d., http://www.rollingstone.com/music/song-stories/rolling-in-the-deep-adele (June 18, 2012).

62. *Sun* (London), "Adele's Rockin' Roll," November 3, 2010, http://www.thesun.co.uk/sol/homepage/showbiz/bizarre/3209467/Adeles-Rolling-back-to-the-top.html?OTC-RSS&ATTR=Bizarre (June 18, 2012).

63–64. Newkey-Burden, *Adele*, 151.

64–65. Ibid., 152.

66. Barry Walters, "Adele, '21,'" *Spin*, February 22, 2011, http://www.spin.com/reviews/adele-21-xlcolumbia (June 18, 2012).

66. Simon Harper, "Adele: 21—All About That Voice," Clash, January 24, 2011, http://www.clashmusic.com/reviews/adele-21 (June 18, 2012).

66–67. Van Meter, "Adele."

69. Newkey-Burden, Adele, 167.

59. Van Meter, "Adele."

71. Guardian (London), "Adele's Tax Grievances Won't Resonate with Fans," May 25, 2011, http://www.guardian.co.uk/music /musicblog/2011/may/25/adele-tax-grievances (June 21, 2012).

74. Shapiro, Adele, 141.

74. Ibid., 142.

75. Ibid., 145.

79. Benjy Eisen, "Adele Cancels U.S. Tour Due to Illness," Rolling Stone, October 4, 2011, http://www.rollingstone.com/music/news /adele-cancels-u-s-tour-due-to-illness-20111004 (June 21, 2012).

79. Van Meter, "Adele."

83. Ibid.

86. Ibid.

86–88. Ibid.

89. Alison Schwartz, "Adele Will Make First Post-Surgery Performance at Grammys," People, January 31, 2012, http://www.peoplestylewatch .com/people/stylewatch/package/article/0,,20552371_20566033,00 .html (June 23, 2012).

90. ABC, "Grammys 2012: Adele Sweeps, Jennifer Hudson Delivers Stirring Tribute to Whitney Houston," ABC News, February 13, 2012, http://abcnews.go.com/Entertainment/grammys-2012-adele- sweeps-jennifer-hudson-delivers-stirring/story?id=15571619# .UDEI9N2PWLI (August 19, 2012).

92. BBC, "Brit Awards: Adele Cut Short Amid Triumph," BBC, February 21, 2012, http://www.bbc.co.uk/news/entertainment- arts-17104569 (June 28, 2012).

94. Seth Abramovitch, "Adele's 'Skyfall' Is Every Inch a Classic Bond Theme," Hollywood Reporter, October 4, 2012, http://www .hollywoodreporter.com/earshot/adeles-leaked-skyfall -bond-theme-376494 (October 8, 2012).

95. Adele, "Blog: I've Got Some News," Adele.tv, June 29, 2012, http://
www.adele.tv/blogcache/i-ve-got-some-news/ (July 1, 2012).

95–96. Van Meter, "Adele."

96. Ibid.

94. Pink, "Adele," Time, April 18, 2012. http://www.time.com/time
/specials/packages/article/0,28804,2111975_2111976_2111950,00
.html (June 29, 2012).

SELECTED BIBLIOGRAPHY

Bates, Daniel. "Why Voice Surgery for Vocal Haemorrhage Did Not Stop Me Swearing, by Adele." *Daily Mail* (London), February 9, 2012. http://www.dailymail.co.uk/tvshowbiz/article-2098512/Singer-Adele-Voice-surgery-vocal-haemorrhage-did-stop-swearing.html (May 17, 2012).

BBC, "Grammy Glory for Returning Adele." *BBC*, February 12, 2012. http://www.bbc.co.uk/news/entertainment-arts-17007642 (May 17, 2012).

Eisen, Benjy. "Adele Cancels U.S. Tour due to Illness." *Rolling Stone*, October 4, 2011. http://www.rollingstone.com/music/news/adele-cancels-u-s-tour-due-to-illness-20111004 (June 21, 2012).

Gunderson, Edna. "Grammys Will be Adele's Vocal 'Debut'." *USA Today*, sect. D-2, February 10, 2012.

Lewis, Pete. "Adele: Up Close and Personal." *B&S*. N.d. http://www.bluesandsoul.com/feature/302/the_futures_looking_rosie_for_adele/ (June 4, 2012).

Newkey-Burden, Chas. *Adele: The Biography*. Croydon, UK: John Blake Publishing, 2011.

Patterson, Sylvia. "Mad about the Girl." *The Guardian* (London), January 26, 2008. http://www.guardian.co.uk/music/2008/jan/27/popandrock.britawards2008 (June 29, 2012).

Shapiro, Marc. *Adele: The Biography*. New York: St. Martin's Press, 2012.

Van Meter, Jonathan. "Adele: One and Only." *Vogue*, February 13, 2012. http://www.vogue.com/magazine/article/adele-one-and-only/#5 (June 21, 2012).

FURTHER READING AND WEBSITES

Books

Bailey, Diane. *Mary J. Blige*. New York: Rosen Publishing Group, 2009. R & B artist Mary J. Blige has been a major influence on many modern artists, including Adele. Learn more about her life and career in this biography.

Hamilton, Jill, ed. *The Music Industry*. Detroit: Greenhaven Press, 2009. This title takes an in-depth look at the modern music industry, its successes, challenges, and future business models.

Handyside, Chris. *Soul and R&B*. Chicago: Heinemann Library, 2006. Handyside explores the musical genres of soul and R & B, looking at their roots, stars, and place in modern music.

Kaplan, Arie. *American Pop: Hit Makers, Superstars, and Dance Revolutionaries*. Minneapolis: Twenty-First Century Books, 2013. Read about the history of pop music in America, major influences on popular music, and modern stars.

Mendelson, Aaron. *American R & B: Gospel Grooves, Funky Drummers, and Soul Power*. Minneapolis: Twenty-First Century Books, 2013. Learn more about American R & B and all the types of music—including soul—that contribute to this classic American genre.

Stone, Tanya Lee. *Ella Fitzgerald*. New York: Viking, 2008. Read more about jazz legend Ella Fitzgerald—a major musical influence on Adele—in this biography.

Uschan, Michael V. *The Blues*. Detroit: Lucent Books, 2012. The blues is a style of music closely associated with soul. Read about blues music and African American history, how the music has evolved, and its resurgence in recent years.

Websites

Adele—Official Site
http://www.adele.tv/home
Get the latest Adele news, read Adele's personal blog, and find out about upcoming concert dates at Adele's official site.

All Music

http://www.allmusic.com

Learn more about soul, jazz, blues, and all kinds of other musical genres at All Music. The site includes music from influencial artists, music reviews, and recommendations.

Billboard—Adele

http://www.billboard.com/artist/adele/810846

Billboard's page on Adele includes her latest charting news, album reviews, and song samples.

MTV—Adele

http://www.mtv.com/artists/adele

MTV's page on Adele includes news, photos, interviews, and links to her videos.

MySpace—Adele

http://www.myspace.com/adelelondon

Check out the site where it all started for Adele. Adele's MySpace page includes photos, music, and more.

XL Recordings

http://www.xlrecordings.com

Find out what's happening at Adele's label, XL Recordings. The site includes the latest news with XL, a record store, and a page devoted just to Adele.

INDEX

PHOTO ACKNOWLEDGMENTS

The images in this book are used with the permission of: GDA via AP Images, p. 1; © Robert Hanashiro/USA TODAY, pp. 3, 15, 21, 23, 34, 43, 47, 52, 64, 80, 84, 88, 89, © Dan MacMedan/USA TODAY, pp. 4, 6, 32, 55; © Splash News, p. 8; MO1 WENN Photos/ Newscom, p. 9; © Terry O'Neill/Getty Images, p. 10; Express Newspapers via AP Images, p. 11 (top); Stephanie Schaerer/ZUMA Press/Newscom, p. 11 (bottom); © Michael Ochs Archives/Stringer/Getty Images, p. 13; © House Of Fame LLC/Michael Ochs Archives/Getty Images, p. 14; © Associated Newspapers/Daily Mail/Rex/Alamy, p. 16; © Dan Kitwood/ Getty Images, p. 17; © Christie Goodwin/Redferns via Getty Images, p. 18; © Dave Etheridge-Barnes/Getty Images, p. 20; © Todd Strand/Independent Picture Service, pp. 24, 25, 31, 87, © Dave Hogan/Getty Images, p. 26 (left); © Gabriel Olsen/FilmMagic/ Getty Images, p. 26 (right); Andre Csillag/Rex USA, p. 28; © Paul Bergen/Redferns/Getty Images, p. 30; © Gareth Cattermole/Getty Images, p. 33; © Lenscap/Alamy, p. 37; AP Photo/Brian Kersey, p. 38; © Jon Furniss/WireImages/Getty Images, pp. 39, 40; © Joe Kohen/WireImage/Getty Images, p. 42; © Erik Freeland/CORBIS SABA, p. 44; Double Click Images/PacificCoast News/Newscom, p. 46; © Dana Edelson/NBC/NBCU Photo Bank via Getty Images, p. 49; © H. Darr Beiser/USA TODAY, p. 50; © Julian Love/AWL Images/ Getty Images, p. 51; © Astrid Stawiarz/Stringer/Getty Images, p. 54 (left); © Julien M. Hekimian/Stringer/Getty Images, p. 54 (right); © Jon Klemm Photography, p. 57; © Lonely Planet/Getty Images, p. 58; © ABC-TV/Feld, Danny/Kobal Collection/Art Resource, NY , p. 59; © Bob Riha Jr./USA TODAY, p. 61; © Studio 101/Alamy, p. 63; © Matt Kent/ WireImages/Getty Images, p. 67; © Joel Ryan/AP/CORBIS, p. 68; © Todd Plitt/USA TODAY, p. 70; JD1 WENN.com/Newscom, p. 71; AP Photo/Robert E. Klein, p. 73; Josephine Santos/PacificCoast News/Newscom, p. 75; AP Photo/Columbia Records, p. 76; © Laura Westlund/Independent Picture Service, p. 78; © Jesse Grant/WireImages/Getty Images, p. 79; AP Photo/Mark Allan, p. 82; © Kevin Mazur/WireImage/Getty Images, p. 86; © Lynn Goldsmith/CORBIS, p. 91; © Dave J Hogan/Getty Images, p. 92; Invicta Kent Media/ Rex USA, p. 93; PRNewsFoto/Columbia Records/AP Photo, p. 95; © Mert Alas and Marcus Piggott/Vogue/AP Photo, p. 96.

Front cover: Matt Baron/BEImages/Rex USA.
Back cover: © Kevin Mazur/WireImage/Getty Images.

Main body text set in USA TODAY Roman Regular 10.5/15.

ABOUT THE AUTHOR

Matt Doeden is a freelance author and editor. He has written hundreds of children's and young adult books covering areas such as sports, the military, cars, history, geography and, of course, music. He lives in Minnesota with his family.